NYSTCE232 Multi-Subject 232 Teachers of Middle Childhood Grade 5–Grade 9

New York State Teacher Certification Examinations®

By: Preparing Teachers In America™

This page is intentionally left blank.

© 2016 by Preparing Teachers In America

Publication by Preparing Teachers In America Publication Services, a division of Preparing Teachers In America

Printed in the United States of America

ISBN-13 978-1537613086

ISBN-10: 1537613081

This page is intentionally left blank.

Free Online Email Tutoring Services

All preparation guides purchased directly from Preparing Teachers In America includes a free three month email tutoring subscription. Any resale of preparation guides does not qualify for a free email tutoring subscription.

What is Email Tutoring?

Email Tutoring allows buyers to send questions to tutors via email. Buyers can send any questions regarding the exam processes, strategies, content questions, or practice questions.

Preparing Teachers In America reserves the right not to answer questions with or without reason(s).

How to use Email Tutoring?

Buyers need to send an email to onlinepreparationservices@gmail.com requesting email tutoring services. Buyers may be required to confirm the email address used to purchase the preparation guide or additional information prior to using email tutoring. Once email tutoring subscription is confirmed, buyers will be provided an email address to send questions to. The three month period will start the day the subscription is confirmed.

Any misuse of email tutoring services will result in termination of service. Preparing Teachers In America reserves the right to terminate email tutoring subscription at anytime with or without notice.

Comments and Suggestions

All comments and suggestions for improvements for the study guide and email tutoring services need to be sent to onlinepreparationservices@gmail.com.

This page is intentionally left blank.

Table of Content

This page is intentionally left blank.

About the Exam and Study Guide

What is the NYSTCE® Middle Grades Mathematics Exam?

The NYSTCE® Middle Grades Mathematics is an exam to measure potential teachers' competencies in mathematics knowledge related to middle school grade levels. The test measures whether individuals have the knowledge necessary to start teaching middle school math. The exam is based largely on teacher preparation standards, and the following are content areas covered by the middle school math exam:

- Number Sense and Operations
- Algebra and Functions
- Measurement and Geometry
- Statistics and Probability

The exam is timed at 75 minutes for the 40 selected-response questions, and the exam is timed at 60 minutes for the constructed response. The selected-response questions and the constructed response are based on knowledge obtained in a bachelor's degree program. The exam contains some questions that may not count toward the score. Calculators are permitted on the exam.

What topics are covered on the exam?

The following are some topics covered on the exam:

- numbers
- operations
- patterns, relations, and functions
- algebraic techniques and applications
- nonlinear relations and concepts of calculus
- measurement principles, procedures, and applications
- geometry in two and three dimensions
- coordinate and transformational geometry
- principles and techniques of statistics
- principles of probability and techniques for determining probability

What is included in this study guide book?

This guide includes two full length practice exams for the NYSTCE® Middle Grades Mathematics along with detail explanations. The recommendation is to take the tests under timed exam conditions and a quiet environment.

This page is intentionally left blank.

Practice Test 1

This page is intentionally left blank.

Exam Answer Sheet – Test 1

Below is an optional answer sheet to use to document answers.

Question Number	Selected Answer	Question Number	Selected Answer
1		21	
2		22	
3		23	
4		24	
5		25	
6		26	
7		27	
8		28	
9		29	
10		30	
11		31	
12		32	
13		33	
14		34	
15		35	
16		36	
17		37	
18		38	
19		39	
20		40	

This page is intentionally left blank.

QUESTION 1

At a high school, the ratio of basketball players to baseball players is 7 to 3, and the ratio of football players to soccer players is 8 to 5. If the ratio of baseball players to soccer players is 1 to 4, then what is the ratio of the basketball players to football players?

A. $\frac{35}{96}$

B. $\frac{7}{8}$

C. $\frac{7}{24}$

D. $\frac{18}{35}$

Answer:

QUESTION 2

If the value in the thousands place of the first number is multiplied with the value in the hundreds place in the second number, and this product is added to the value in the thousandths place of the third number, then what number will result from these operations?

Number 1: 124,587

Number 2: 25,478.2445

Number 3: 145.25402

A. 39

B. 35

C. 20

D. 16

Answer:

QUESTION 3

Which of the following reflections is done across the line y = – x?

A. P(x, y) --> P'(x, – y)

B. P(x, y) --> P'(– x, y)

C. P(x, y) --> P'(y, x)

D. P(x, y) --> P'(– y, – x)

Answer:

QUESTION 4

If the value of t, in the equation below, is increased by 2, how will the value of g change?

$$g = 4 \times (t + 2)^2 + 3 \times (t+p) - 5$$

A. 25

B. 16t + 54

C. 16t + 4p + 54

D. 54

Answer:

QUESTION 5

The position of a particle moving in an accelerator is given by $p(t) = 2t^3 - 4t^2 + 2t - 1$. What is the position of the particle at $t = 4$ seconds?

    A. 23

    B. 43

    C. 71

    D. 7943

Answer:

QUESTION 6

Two trapezoids are shown in the figure below. Trapezoid 1 has height of 8 in, a base of 10 in, and an area of 148 in^2. Trapezoid 2 has height of 16 in and a base of 20 in. If the two trapezoids are similar, what is the length of the other base in Trapezoid 2?

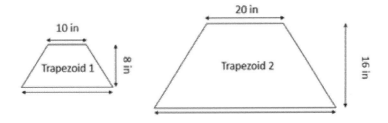

    A. 12 in

    B. 27 in

    C. 54 in

    D. Not enough information

Answer:

QUESTION 7

In the figure below, angle A is equal to x – 24 degrees. If angle B is equal to x – 36 degrees, then what is the value of x?

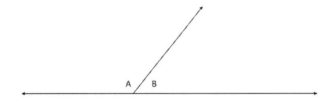

    A. 84°

    B. 86°

    C. 120°

    D. 180°

Answer:

QUESTION 8

A university counselor was asked to report on the number of students enrolled in the five different colleges at the university. The counselor was asked to also report on the number of males and females in each of those five colleges. The data the counselor obtained is shown below. Which of the following graphs accurately represent the data obtained?

	Males	Females	Total
College of Business	250	300	550
College of Engineering	162	85	247
College of Liberal Arts	144	225	369
College of Natural Sciences	325	336	661
College of Technology	114	96	210

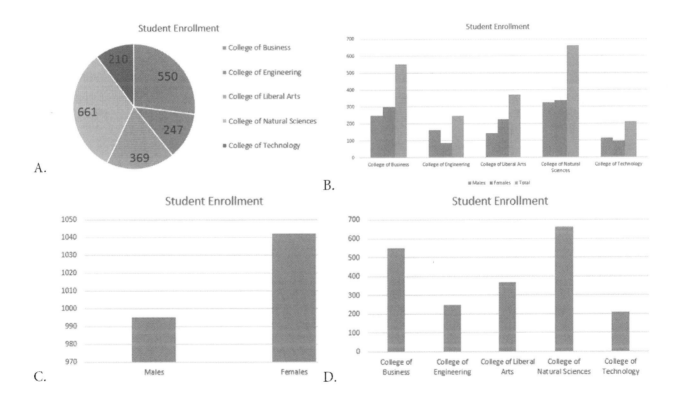

A.

B.

C.

D.

Answer:

One letter will be randomly selected from the set below. What is the probability that is a vowel or precedes the letter G in alphabetical order?

$$\{A, B, C, L, M, N, O, P, E, F, H, I, T, S, V, U\}$$

A. 0.0977

B. 0.3125

C. 0.5000

D. 0.6250

Answer:

QUESTION 10

Considering the Venn diagram below, which of the following options is true?

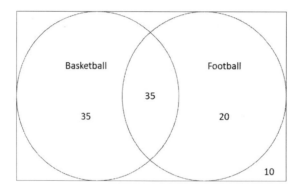

A. P(Basketball) < P(Football)

B. P(Basketball and Football) < P(Football)

C. P(Basketball and Football) > P(Basketball)

D. P(Basketball or Football) = 1.00

Answer:

QUESTION 11

Point A is located at (4, 6) and is to be shifted three units to the left and four units downward. After this translation, the point is rotated 270° about the origin. What is the location of this point after these transformations?

    A. (2, -1)

    B. (1, 2)

    C. (-1, -2)

    D. (-2, 1)

Answer:

QUESTION 12

Ronald, George and James have each ordered a pizza. Ronald's pizza is 30% larger than George's pizza. James' pizza is 30% larger than George's pizza. Ronald has eaten 37.5% of his pizza. George has about 0.05 of his pizza remaining. James has eaten $\frac{3}{7}$ of his pizza. Approximately, which of the following correctly orders who has eaten the most pizza?

    A. Ronald > James > George

    B. George > James > Ronald

    C. James > George> Ronald

    D. Ronald > George > James

Answer:

QUESTION 13

Set S contains the following numbers. Which of the following options lists the rational numbers of the set in order from least to greatest?

$$S = \{-1.25 \times 10^{-4}, 5.2 \times 10^{3}, 0.111, 1.75, \sqrt{2}, \sqrt{-25}, \sqrt{4}, \sqrt{25}, 1.25 \times 10^{-5}, 125478, 145\sqrt{2}, \sqrt{5.2 \times 10^{3}}\}$$

A. $\{\sqrt{-25}, -1.25 \times 10^{-4}, 1.25 \times 10^{-5}, 0.111, 1.75, \sqrt{4}, \sqrt{25}, \sqrt{5.2 \times 10^{3}}, 5.2 \times 10^{3}, 125478\}$

B. $\{-1.25 \times 10^{-4}, 1.25 \times 10^{-5}, 0.111, 1.75, \sqrt{2}, \sqrt{4}, \sqrt{25}, \sqrt{5.2 \times 10^{3}}, 5.2 \times 10^{3}, 125478\}$

C. $\{-1.25 \times 10^{-4}, 1.25 \times 10^{-5}, 0.111, 1.75, \sqrt{4}, \sqrt{25}, \sqrt{5.2 \times 10^{3}}, 5.2 \times 10^{3}, 125478\}$

D. $\{1.25 \times 10^{-5}, -1.25 \times 10^{-4}, 0.111, 1.75, \sqrt{4}, \sqrt{25}, \sqrt{5.2 \times 10^{3}}, 5.2 \times 10^{3}, 125478\}$

Answer:

QUESTION 14

A bucket consists of red and blue marbles. The red marbles weigh 2 grams and the blue marble weigh 7 grams. The total weight of the bucket is 85 grams. If it is known that there are 2 more red marbles than blue marbles, then what is the total number of marbles in the bucket?

A. 8

B. 9

C. 18

D. 20

Answer:

QUESTION 15

At time 0, Chris leaves work and heads home. The following graphs shows the distance Chris is from work as time goes by. During the period between 1 and 5 minutes, which of the following best describes what Chris was doing?

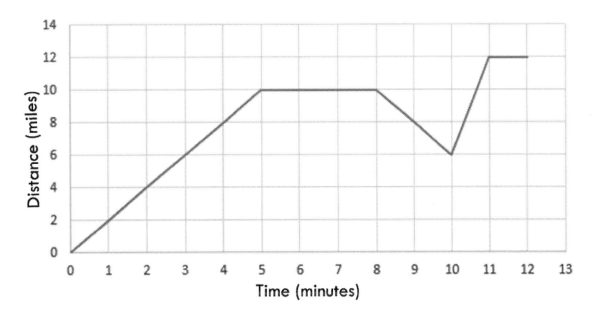

A. Chris is stuck in traffic and is not moving.

B. Chris is heading in a direction towards his workplace.

C. Chris is heading home at a constant speed.

D. Chris has parked his car in his driveway.

Answer:

QUESTION 16

Which of the given equations has the following three zeros and passes through the x values below?

$$x = -1, x = 2, \text{ and } x = -6$$

A. $f(x) = x^2 - x - 2$

B. $f(x) = 2x - x^2$

C. $f(x) = 2x^3 + 10x^2 - 16x - 24$

D. $f(x) = x^3 - 7x^2 + 4x + 12$

Answer:

QUESTION 17

How many zeros does the function in the graph below show?

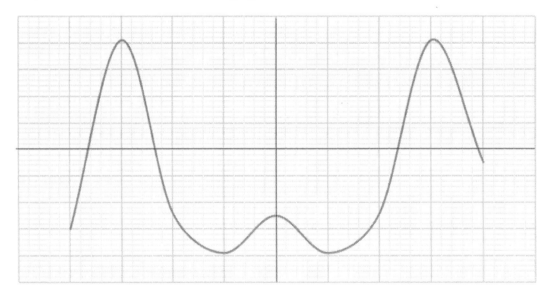

A. 1

B. 2

C. 3

D. 4

Answer:

QUESTION 18

Select the answer choice that does NOT equal to the following rational expression:

$$\frac{m^2 + 9m + 18}{m^2 - m - 12}$$

A. $\dfrac{(m + 3) \times (m + 6)}{(m - 4) \times (m + 3)}$

B. $\dfrac{(m + 6)}{(m - 4)}$

C. $\dfrac{m^2 + 18 + 9m}{m^2 - 12 - m}$

D. $\left(\dfrac{m^2 + 9m + 18}{m^2 - m - 12}\right)^{-1}$

Answer:

QUESTION 19

Which of the following options is false?

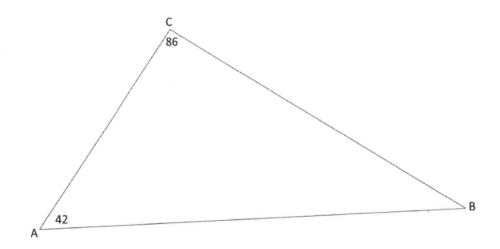

A. ∢CAB <∢CBA <∢BCA

B. $\overline{BC}$< $\overline{CA}$<$\overline{BA}$

C. ∢CAB + ∢CBA + ∢BCA = 180

D. $\overline{BA}$>$\overline{BC}$>$\overline{CA}$

Answer:

QUESTION 20

A chair manufacturer can build a maximum of 200 chairs in one month. The manufacturer takes orders of 5 chairs per order. For the month of March, the manufacturer has already secured orders for a total of 120 chairs. What is the maximum number of orders the manufacturer can add to the production for March?

A. 16

B. 40

C. 80

D. 120

Answer:

QUESTION 21

Which number line below graphically represents the answer to the following inequality?

$$|4x + 12| < 2x + 12$$

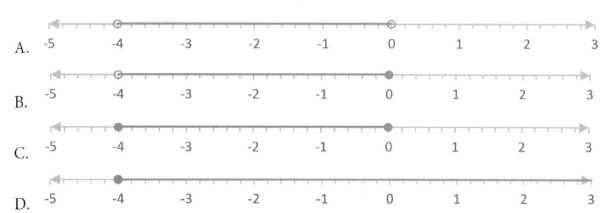

A.

B.

C.

D.

Answer:

QUESTION 22

Which of the following options is a median for the isosceles triangle shown below?

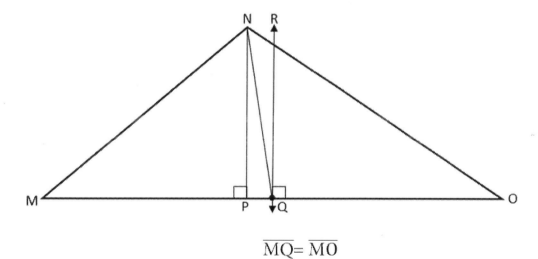

$$\overline{MQ} = \overline{MO}$$

A. $\overline{NP}$

B. $\overleftrightarrow{RQ}$

C. $\overline{NQ}$

D. $\overline{MQ}$

Answer:

QUESTION 23

Which of the following sets of numbers cannot be the measurements of the sides of a triangle?

    A. 6, 8, and 10

    B. 9, 12, and 22

    C. 7, 13, and 19

    D. 12, 19, and 25

Answer:

QUESTION 24

John has been told by his parents that he can no longer spend more than $100 per month. In the first week of the month, John spent $14 on a movie ticket. In the second week, John spend $12 at the arcade. In the third week, John chose not to spend any money, so he could spend more the following week at his friend's birthday party. Which of the following number lines most accurately shows how much money John can spend in the last week of the month?

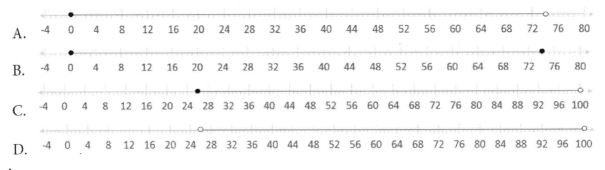

Answer:

QUESTION 25

A mechanic charges $50 an hour to fix a car and requires 65% reimbursement of any additional costs needed to fix the car. If the mechanic had to purchase $350 worth of the equipment to fix the car, how much of this cost will be paid back to the mechanic.

    A. $122.50

    B. $227.50

    C. $277.50

    D. $350.00

Answer:

QUESTION 26

If $a < b < -1 < 0 < 1 < c < d$, then which of the following fractions has the smallest value?

    A. $\dfrac{b}{a}$

    B. $\dfrac{c}{d}$

    C. $\dfrac{0}{c}$

    D. $\dfrac{d}{b}$

Answer:

QUESTION 27

What digit will be in the hundreds place of 1.25468×10^{25}?

    A. 0

    B. 6

    C. 5

    D. 2

Answer:

QUESTION 28

In parallelogram MNOP, $\angle M = x + 15$ and $\angle N = 3x + 5$. What is the value of $\angle P$?

Answer:

QUESTION 29

What is the result of performing this multiplication?

$$(-15 + 3i) \times (5 + 4i)$$

    A. -87 – 45i

    B. -87 – 33i

    C. -63 – 45i

    D. -63 – 33i

Answer:

QUESTION 30

What value(s) of x will satisfy the following equation?

$$18x^2 + 24x + 8 = 0$$

    A. 0

    B. -2/3

    C. 2/3

    D. 2/3 and -2/3

Answer:

QUESTION 31

John's weekly income consists of his hourly wages and a $50 weekly allowance given to him by his father. Maria's weekly income consists of her hourly wages and a weekly allowance given to her by her father. John earns $10 an hour and Maria earns $12 an hour. If they each work for 10 hours in one week, how much weekly allowance does Maria's father need to give her, so both Maria and John earn the same income in that week?

   A. $20

   B. $30

   C. $50

   D. $120

Answer:

QUESTION 32

Solve for x and y:

$$12x + 12y = 40$$
$$8x + 4y = 32$$

   A. $x = -11\frac{1}{3}$ and $y = 14\frac{2}{3}$

   B. $x = -1\frac{5}{9}$ and $y = 4\frac{8}{9}$

   C. $x = 4\frac{2}{3}$ and $y = -8\frac{1}{3}$

   D. $x = 4\frac{2}{3}$ and $y = -1\frac{1}{3}$

Answer:

QUESTION 33

The graph below represents the solution to which of the following inequalities

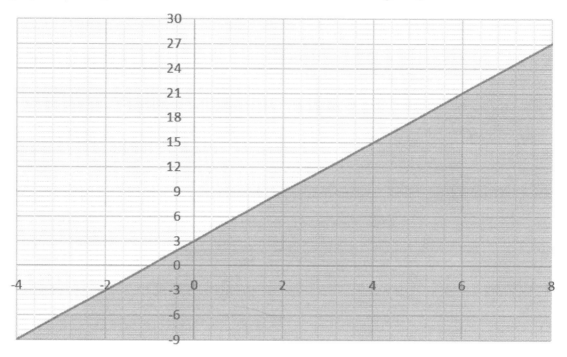

A. $y < -3x - 3$

B. $y \le 3x + 3$

C. $y < 3x + 3$

D. $y \ge 3x + 3$

Answer:

QUESTION 34

What are the next three numbers in the following sequence?

10, 40, 160, 640

  A. 2560, 10240, 40960

  B. 10240, 40960, 163840,

  C. 10, 40, 160

  D. 640, 2560, 10240

Answer:

QUESTION 35

Given $f(x) = 5x + 20$ and $g(x) = 6x + 12$, what is $f(g(3))$?

  A. 30

  B. 35

  C. 170

  D. 222

Answer:

QUESTION 36

In his algebra class, John's professor assigns 3 group projects and 3 exams. The three group projects are worth 20%, 25%, and 20%, respectively, of the final course grade. The three exams are worth 10%, 15%, and 10% of the final course grade. If John earned a 73, 75, and 97 on the group projects, respectively, and a 99, 93, and 100 on the exams, respectively, then what is his final course grade?

  A. 91.3

  B. 89.5

  C. 86.6

  D. 78.2

Answer:

QUESTION 37

The owner of a local gym asked people in the community how many hours they work out during the week. The owner recorded his results in the line plot below. What is the median, mode, and range of the data set?

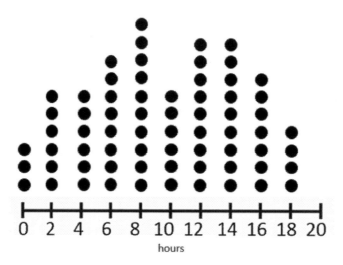

A. Median = 8; Mode = 10; Range = 20

B. Median = 9; Mode = 8; Range = 18

C. Median = 10; Mode = 8; Range = 1

D. Median = 16; Mode = 10; Range = 16

Answer:

QUESTION 38

What of the following scenarios can be modeled by the line graph shown below?

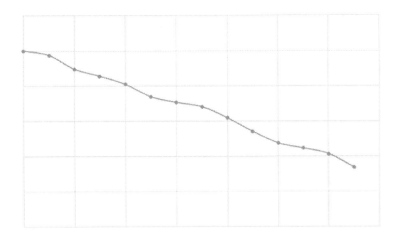

A. At the end of every year, Marcus takes his car to the dealership. The mechanic at the dealership performs the annual check-ups and tells Marcus the market value of the car. Marcus takes the value of the car at the end of each year and creates a line graph.

B. Michael takes out a loan from a bank. He pays off equal portions of the loan every month. Michael wants to create a line graph that shows the value of loan he had remaining at the end of each month that he made a payment in.

C. Maria takes out a loan from a bank. She pays off equal portions of the loan every month. Maria wants to create a line graph that shows the cumulative sum of money she has given to the bank at the end of each month.

D. A and B

Answer:

QUESTION 39

The following pie chart breaks down several of the expenses for a grocery store in a given year. If a total of $923,800 was spent on wages, how much money was spent on taxes and physical capital?

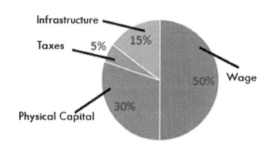

A. $1,847,600

B. $646,660

C. $554,280

D. $92,380

Answer:

QUESTION 40

Marissa's neighbors have 3 dogs. What is the probability that two of the three dogs are male?

A. 0.875

B. 0.500

C. 0.375

D. 0.250

Answer:

Constructed Response 1

Use the data provided to complete the task that follows.

Using the data provided, prepare a response of approximately 400–600 words in which you:

- identify an important mathematical strength related to the standard that is demonstrated by the student, citing specific evidence from the exhibits to support your assessment;
- identify an important area of need related to the standard that is demonstrated by the student, citing specific evidence from the exhibits to support your assessment; and
- describe an instructional plan that builds on the student's strengths and that would help the student improve in the identified area of need. Include a plan for assisting the student build a viable argument related to the given standard.

Eighth-grade students have been developing their understanding functions and modeling relationships between quantities. The class is currently working on the following standard from the New York State P–12 Common Core Learning Standards for Mathematics:

CCSS.Math.Content.8.F.B.4

Construct a function to model a linear relationship between two quantities. Determine the rate of change and initial value of the function from a description of a relationship or from two (x, y) values, including reading these from a table or from a graph. Interpret the rate of change and initial value of a linear function in terms of the situation it models, and in terms of its graph or a table of values.

Description of Class Activity

The teacher pairs students and has the students complete the following activity:

A company is going to buy new manufacturing units. Brand A costs $250,000 to buy and $10,000 a month to operate. Brand B costs $450,000 to buy, but only cost $4,000 a month to operate.

Use a system of linear equations to analyze the cost of purchasing and operating each of these two brands. Your response should show all work and include:

A. a particular equation for each unit expressing the total cost of operation as a function of the number of months since the purchase of the unit;
B. a sketch of the graphs of the two equations on one set of coordinate axes, with the axes, scales, intercepts, and any calculated points clearly labeled;
C. an explanation of the slope and intercepts of each function in the context of the problem situation;
D. calculation of the "break-even" point for the two functions, i.e., the number of months for which the total cost of the two units would be the same; and
E. advice for the company as to which would be the less expensive option.

Excerpt of Student's Work
Part B

Both equations are linear, so just two points are needed per graph. For Brand A, choose the initial point when t=0, and a point down the line, let's say t=100 months. The data points for Brand A are shown in the table below.

Time (months)	Work	Total Cost ($)
0	Brand A = $10,000(0) + $250,000	250,000
100	Brand A = $10,000(100) + $250,000	1,250,000

Similarly for Brand B, the data points are shown in the table below.

Time (months)	Work	Total Cost ($)
0	Brand B = $4,000(0) + $450,000	450,000
100	Brand B = $4,000(100) + $450,000	850,000

Sketch both lines in the same graph by connecting the points.

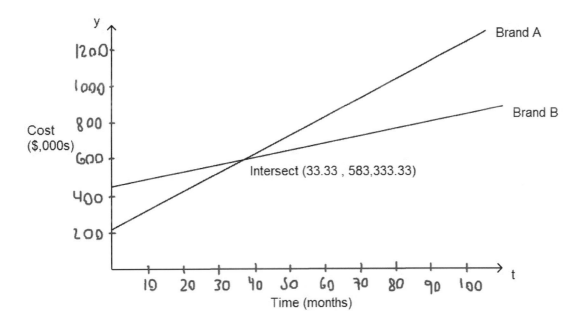

Excerpt of Conversation With Teacher

Teacher: What did you used to graph the lines?

Student: I used the information in the question to draw the graph.

Teacher: What specifically did you used to draw the lines?

Student: Brand A cost $250,000, so when it is 0 months that will be the value on the y-axis.

Teacher: Is that the y-intercept?

Student: Yes

Teacher: What else did you used?

Student: Brand B cost $450,000, so when it is 0 months that will be the value on the y-axis.

Teacher: Anything else you used to graph the lines?

Student: There is increase of $10,000 for Brand A and $4,000 for Brand B, so I just increased roughly that amount each month.

Teacher: Can you tell me the slope values for these equations?

Student: The slope is going to be the x-intercept values.

Middle School Practice Exam Answers – Test 1

Question Number	Selected Answer	Question Number	Selected Answer
1	A	21	A
2	C	22	C
3	D	23	B
4	B	24	B
5	B	25	B
6	C	26	D
7	C	27	A
8	B	28	125
9	C	29	A
10	B	30	B
11	A	31	B
12	B	32	D
13	C	33	B
14	D	34	A
15	C	35	C
16	C	36	C
17	D	37	B
18	D	38	A
19	D	39	B
20	A	40	D

NOTE: Getting approximately 80% of the questions correct increases chances of obtaining passing score on the real exam. This varies from different states and university programs.

This page is intentionally left blank.

QUESTION 1

At a high school, the ratio of basketball players to baseball players is 7 to 3, and the ratio of football players to soccer players is 8 to 5. If the ratio of baseball players to soccer players is 1 to 4, then what is the ratio of the basketball players to football players?

A. $\frac{35}{96}$

B. $\frac{7}{8}$

C. $\frac{7}{24}$

D. $\frac{18}{35}$

Answer: A

Explanation: The best approach is to write the ratios in fraction form; this is shown below

$$\frac{\text{basketball}}{\text{baseball}} = \frac{7}{3}, \frac{\text{football}}{\text{soccer}} = \frac{8}{5}, \frac{\text{baseball}}{\text{soccer}} = \frac{1}{4}$$

To find the ratio of basketball players to the football players, the ratio of basketball players to baseball players needs to be multiplied by the ratio of baseball players to soccer players. Then, the result needs to be multiplied by the inverse of the ratio of football players to soccer players. These operations are summarized below:

$$\frac{\text{basketball}}{\text{baseball}} \times \frac{\text{baseball}}{\text{soccer}} \times \frac{\text{soccer}}{\text{football}}$$

$$\frac{7}{3} \times \frac{1}{4} \times \frac{5}{8} = \frac{35}{96}$$

The result of the operations shows that the ratio of basketball players to football players is $\frac{35}{96}$.

QUESTION 2

If the value in the thousands place of the first number is multiplied with the value in the hundreds place in the second number, and this product is added to the value in the thousandths place of the third number, then what number will result from these operations?

Number 1: 124,587

Number 2: 25,478.2445

Number 3: 145.25402

A. 39

B. 35

C. 20

D. 16

Answer: C

Explanation: The first number has 6 digits. The digit in the thousands place is the value 4 places to the left of the decimal point. The first number does not have a decimal point, so it is assumed to be at the end of the number. Thus, the value in the thousands place of the first number is 4. The second number has 5 digits to the left of the decimal point and 4 digits to the right of the decimal point. The digit in the hundreds place is the value 3 places to the left of the decimal point. Thus, the value in the hundreds place of the second number is 4. The first operation to be performed is the multiplication of the value in the thousands place of the first number and the value in the hundreds place in the second number. This operation results in 4 x 4 =16. The second operation required the addition of 16 and the value in the thousandths place of the third number. The third number has 3 digits to the left of the decimal point and 5 digits to the right of the decimal point. The thousandths place is the value 3 places to the right of the decimal point. Thus, the value in the thousandths place of the third number is 4. The addition of 4 to 16 results in 20.

QUESTION 3

Which of the following reflections is done across the line y = – x?

    A. P(x, y) --> P'(x, – y)

    B. P(x, y) --> P'(– x, y)

    C. P(x, y) --> P'(y, x)

    D. P(x, y) --> P'(– y, – x)

Answer: D

Explanation: To answer the question, it is important to know the changes in the x-coordinate and y-coordinate of a point when it is reflected across the x-axis, y-axis, y = x, and y = – x.

- When a point is reflected across the x-axis, the x-coordinate remains the same and the y coordinate is multiplied by – 1.
- When a point is reflected across the y-axis, the x-coordinate is multiplied by – 1 and the y coordinate remains the same.
- When a point is reflected across the line y = x, the x-coordinate and y-coordinate change places.
- When a point is reflected across the line y = – x, the x-coordinate and y-coordinate change places and each are also multiplied by -1.

Of the options shown, only Option D shows a reflection across the line y = -x.

QUESTION 4

If the value of t, in the equation below, is increased by 2, how will the value of g change?

$$g = 4 \times (t + 2)^2 + 3 \times (t+p) - 5$$

A. 25

B. 16t + 54

C. 16t + 4p + 54

D. 54

Answer: B

Explanation: The best approach to this problem is to first expand the equation given. The expansion results in the following expression:

$$g = 4 \times (t + 2)^2 + 3 \times (t+p) - 5 = 4t^2 + 19t + 3p + 11$$

The next step is to input (t+2) for the variable t in the expression above. This results in the following:

$$g = 4t^2 + 19t + 3p + 11 = 4(t + 2)^2 + 19(t + 2) + 3p + 11 = 4t^2 + 35t + 3p + 65$$

The final step is to subtract the original expression obtained from the new expression to see the effect of adding 2 to the value of t. This is shown below:

$$(4t^2 + 35t + 3p + 65) - (4t^2 + 19t + 3p + 11) = 16t + 54$$

QUESTION 5

The position of a particle moving in an accelerator is given by $p(t) = 2t^3 - 4t^2 + 2t - 1$. What is the position of the particle at t = 4 seconds?

    A. 23

    B. 43

    C. 71

    D. 7943

Answer: B

Explanation: The answer will come after substituting 4 for the variable t in the formula for the position.

$p(2) = 2 \times (4^3) - 4 \times (4^2) + 2 \times (4) - 1 = 2 \times (64) - 4 \times (16) + 2 \times (4) - 1 = 128 - 64 + 8 - 1 = 71$

QUESTION 6

Two trapezoids are shown in the figure below. Trapezoid 1 has height of 8 in, a base of 10 in, and an area of 148 in². Trapezoid 2 has height of 16 in and a base of 20 in. If the two trapezoids are similar, what is the length of the other base in Trapezoid 2?

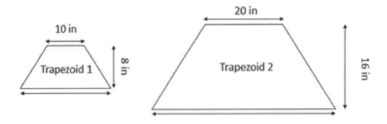

   A. 12 in

   B. 27 in

   C. 54 in

   D. Not enough information

Answer: C

Explanation: To determine the length of the second base in Trapezoid 2, its area needs to be calculated. Since the two trapezoids are similar, its area will be determined by taking into account the ratios between the side lengths of the two trapezoids. The ratio of the areas of two similar polygons equals the square of the ratios of the lengths of any two corresponding sides. The lengths of the top bases of each trapezoid can be used to determine the ratio of the areas of the two trapezoids, as shown below.

$$\frac{A_{T1}}{A_{T2}} = \left(\frac{10}{20}\right)^2 = \frac{1}{4}$$

The area of Trapezoid 2 will be 4 times the area of Trapezoid 1; this is calculated to be 592 inches². With the area of Trapezoid 2 known, along with the length of the height and one base, the length of the other base can be calculated, as shown below.

$$A_{T2} = \frac{1}{2} \times h \times (b_1 + b_2) = 592 = \frac{1}{2} \times 16 \times (20 + b_2) \rightarrow b_2 = 54 \text{ inches}$$

QUESTION 7

In the figure below, angle A is equal to x – 24 degrees. If angle B is equal to x – 36 degrees, then what is the value of x?

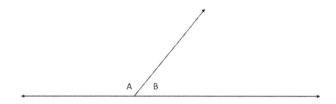

    A. 84°

    B. 86°

    C. 120°

    D. 180°

Answer: C

Explanation: The figure shows the sum of angles A and B must equal 180 degrees. To solve this problem, the given values of angles A, and B are added and set equal to 180°. This creates an equation with one unknown variable, which can be solved for.

$$\angle A + \angle B = x - 24 + x - 36 = 2x - 60 = 180° \rightarrow x = 120°$$

QUESTION 8

A university counselor was asked to report on the number of students enrolled in the five different colleges at the university. The counselor was asked to also report on the number of males and females in each of those five colleges. The data the counselor obtained is shown below. Which of the following graphs accurately represent the data obtained?

	Males	Females	Total
College of Business	250	300	550
College of Engineering	162	85	247
College of Liberal Arts	144	225	369
College of Natural Sciences	325	336	661
College of Technology	114	96	210

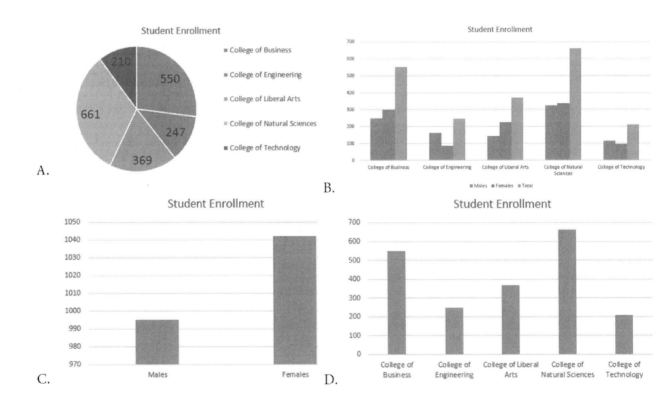

Answer: B

Explanation: The counselor is asked to report on data that can be broken down into qualitative categories, so the best representation of the data will be a bar graph. Since the counselor was asked to report on the total enrollment in each college and also the distribution of the enrollment size by gender, the best representation is shown in option B. Option B is correct because anyone viewing the graph can read the total number of students in each college and also the number of males and females in each college. The other options do not convey these three sets of information all at once.

QUESTION 9

One letter will be randomly selected from the set below. What is the probability that is a vowel or precedes the letter G in alphabetical order?

$$\{A, B, C, L, M, N, O, P, E, F, H, I, T, S, V, U\}$$

    A. 0.0977

    B. 0.3125

    C. 0.5000

    D. 0.6250

Answer: C

Explanation: There are a total of 16 letters given in the set. Of the 16 letters, 5 are vowels. Thus, the probability of selecting a vowel is $\frac{5}{16} = 0.3125$. Of the 16 letters, 5 letters precede the letter G, and, of these 5 letters, only 3 are not vowels. Thus, the probability of selecting a letter that precedes the letter G is $\frac{3}{16} = 0.1875$. The probability of either of these events occurring is 0.3125 + 0.1875=0.50.

NOTE: Only three of the five letters preceding letter G are considered because the other 2 are represented in the probability of selecting a vowel.

QUESTION 10

Considering the Venn diagram below, which of the following options is true?

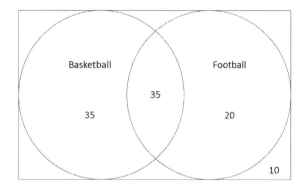

A. P(Basketball) < P(Football)

B. P(Basketball and Football) < P(Football)

C. P(Basketball and Football) > P(Basketball)

D. P(Basketball or Football) = 1.00

Answer: B

Explanation: To answer this question, each of the answer choices needs to be evaluated.

In option A, it is stated that the probability of football is greater than the probability of basketball. However, the probability of basketball is 0.70 and the probability of football is 0.55; which contradicts the statement in option A.

In option B, it is stated that the probability of basketball and football is greater than the probability of football. The probability of basketball and football is 0.35, and the probability of football is 0.55. This option is true.

In option C, it is stated that the probability of basketball and football is greater than the probability of basketball. The probability of basketball and football is 0.35, and the probability of basketball is 0.70. This option is not true.

In option D, it is stated the probability of basketball or football is equal to 1.00. This not true because the probability of basketball or football is equal to 0.70 + 0.55 – 0.35=0.90.

QUESTION 11

Point A is located at (4, 6) and is to be shifted three units to the left and four units downward. After this translation, the point is rotated 270° about the origin. What is the location of this point after these transformations?

    A. (2, -1)

    B. (1, 2)

    C. (-1, -2)

    D. (-2, 1)

Answer: A

Explanation: A shift of three units to the left will decrease the x-coordinate value by three. For Point A, a shift three units to the left results in an x-coordinate value of 1.

A shift four units downward will decrease the y-coordinate value by four. For Point A, a shift four units downward results in a y-coordinate value of 2.

After the shifts, Point A is located at (1, 2).

A rotation of 270° causes the x coordinates and y coordinates to change places and for the y-coordinate to be multiplied by -1: P (x, y) -> P (-y, x). This effect is seen in option A.

QUESTION 12

Ronald, George and James have each ordered a pizza. Ronald's pizza is 30% larger than George's pizza. James' pizza is 30% larger than George's pizza. Ronald has eaten 37.5% of his pizza. George has about 0.05 of his pizza remaining. James has eaten $\frac{3}{7}$ of his pizza. Approximately, which of the following correctly orders who has eaten the most pizza?

    A. Ronald > James > George

    B. George > James > Ronald

    C. James > George > Ronald

    D. Ronald > George > James

Answer: B

Explanation:

The best approach to this problem is to assume that the size of George's pizza is x.

    Ronald's pizza is 30% larger than George's pizza, so the size of his pizza is 1.3x.

    James' pizza is 30% larger than George's pizza, so the size of his pizza is 1.3x.

Now that the size of each person's pizza is known, the next approach is to determine the amount of pizza each has eaten.

    The problem statement says Ronald has eaten 37.5% of his pizza, so he has eaten a total of $1.3x \times 37.5\% = 0.4875x$.

    The problem statement says George has 0.05 of his pizza remaining, so he has eaten a total of $x - 0.05x = 0.95x$.

    The problem statement says James has eaten $\frac{3}{7}$ of his pizza, so he has eaten a total of $1.3x \times \frac{3}{7} = 0.557x$.

George has eaten the most pizza, and Ronald has eaten the least, so the correct answer is B.

QUESTION 13

Set S contains the following numbers. Which of the following options lists the rational numbers of the set in order from least to greatest?

$$S = \{-1.25 \times 10^{-4}, 5.2 \times 10^{3}, 0.111, 1.75, \sqrt{2}, \sqrt{-25}, \sqrt{4}, \sqrt{25}, 1.25 \times 10^{-5}, 125478, 145\sqrt{2}, \sqrt{5.2 \times 10^{3}}\}$$

A. $\{\sqrt{-25}, -1.25 \times 10^{-4}, 1.25 \times 10^{-5}, 0.111, 1.75, \sqrt{4}, \sqrt{25}, \sqrt{5.2 \times 10^{3}}, 5.2 \times 10^{3}, 125478\}$

B. $\{-1.25 \times 10^{-4}, 1.25 \times 10^{-5}, 0.111, 1.75, \sqrt{2}, \sqrt{4}, \sqrt{25}, \sqrt{5.2 \times 10^{3}}, 5.2 \times 10^{3}, 125478\}$

C. $\{-1.25 \times 10^{-4}, 1.25 \times 10^{-5}, 0.111, 1.75, \sqrt{4}, \sqrt{25}, \sqrt{5.2 \times 10^{3}}, 5.2 \times 10^{3}, 125478\}$

D. $\{1.25 \times 10^{-5}, -1.25 \times 10^{-4}, 0.111, 1.75, \sqrt{4}, \sqrt{25}, \sqrt{5.2 \times 10^{3}}, 5.2 \times 10^{3}, 125478\}$

Answer: C

Explanation: The first step is to distinguish which of the numbers in the set are rational numbers and which are not. The rational numbers are:

$$\{-1.25 \times 10^{-4}, 5.2 \times 10^{3}, 0.111, 1.75, \sqrt{4}, \sqrt{25}, 1.25 \times 10^{-5}, 125478, \sqrt{5.2 \times 10^{3}}\}$$

This automatically proves that options A and B are incorrect.

The next step is to arrange the selected numbers from least to greatest. The result is shown below

$$\{-1.25 \times 10^{-4}, 1.25 \times 10^{-5}, 0.111, 1.75, \sqrt{4}, \sqrt{25}, \sqrt{5.2 \times 10^{3}}, 5.2 \times 10^{3}, 125478\}$$

QUESTION 14

A bucket consists of red and blue marbles. The red marbles weigh 2 grams and the blue marble weigh 7 grams. The total weight of the bucket is 85 grams. If it is known that there are 2 more red marbles than blue marbles, then what is the total number of marbles in the bucket?

    A. 8

    B. 9

    C. 18

    D. 20

Answer: D

Explanation: This problem requires setting up a system of equations that model the number of marbles in the bucket and the weight of the bucket.

The number of red marbles can be defined with variable r. The number of blue marbles can be defined with variable b. The total number of marbles is $r + b$. It is known that there are 2 more red marbles than blue marbles, so $r = 2 + b$.

The weight of single red marble is 2 grams, so the weight of r red marbles is 2r. The weight of a single blue marble is 7 grams, so the weight of b blue marbles is 7b. The total weight of b blue marbles and r red marbles can be defined as $7b + 2r$. The problem states that the total weight of the marbles is 85 grams, so the total weight can be expressed as $7b + 2r = 85$. Substituting the expression of $r = 2 + b$ into $7b + 2r = 85$ can yield the value of b. The substitution results in $7b + 2(2 + b) = 85$, which yields a value of 9 for b.

$$7b + 4 + 2b = 85$$

$$9b = 81$$

$$b = 9$$

The analysis above yields a total number of 9 blue marbles and 11 red marbles. There are a total of 20 marbles.

QUESTION 15

At time 0, Chris leaves work and heads home. The following graphs shows the distance Chris is from work as time goes by. During the period between 1 and 5 minutes, which of the following best describes what Chris was doing?

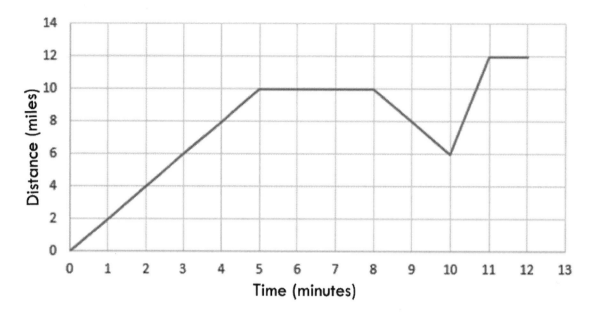

A. Chris is stuck in traffic and is not moving.

B. Chris is heading in a direction towards his workplace.

C. Chris is heading home at a constant speed.

D. Chris has parked his car in his driveway.

Answer: C

Explanation: Between 1 and 5 minutes, the line modeling his distance with respect to time changes constantly. This line implies a constant change in distance with respect to time. Since the ratio of distance to time is considered to be the speed, the line implies he is heading home at a constant speed. Option C is correct.

QUESTION 16

Which of the given equations has the following three zeros and passes through the x values below?

$$x = -1, x = 2, \text{ and } x = -6$$

A. $f(x) = x^2 - x - 2$

B. $f(x) = 2x - x^2$

C. $f(x) = 2x^3 + 10x^2 - 16x - 24$

D. $f(x) = x^3 - 7x^2 + 4x + 12$

Answer: C

Explanation: The problem gives three zeros of a function, which implies the function is a cubic function. This eliminates answer choices A and B. When solving for the zeros of a polynomial, the polynomial is usually factored and each factor is set to equal zero. In this problem, the zeros are already given, so it is best to work backwards.

$x = -1$ implies that the equation has a factor of $(x + 1)$ because $x + 1 = 0$ results in $x = -1$

$x = 2$ implies that the equation has a factor of $(x - 2)$ because $x - 2 = 0$ results in $x = 2$

$x = -6$ implies that the equation has a factor of $(x + 6)$ because $x + 6 = 0$ results in $x = -6$

The three factors of the cubic function can be used to obtain the general form of the family of cubic functions that have the zeros given in the problem statement. The three given zeros can be used only to obtain the general solution because any constant factor can be multiplied to each term in the equation and still result in the same zeros. The general form of the family of cubic functions that results from multiplying the three factors is shown below. Only answer choice C can belong in this family. Answer choice C is the result of multiplying the general form by a value of 2. Answer choice D is not a member of this family.

$$(x + 1) \times (x - 2) = x^2 - x - 2$$

$$(x^2 - x - 2) \times (x + 6) = x^3 + 5x^2 - 8x - 12$$

General form of the family of cubic functions: $a \times (x^3 + 5x^2 - 8x - 12)$

where a is any non-zero number

QUESTION 17

How many zeros does the function in the graph below show?

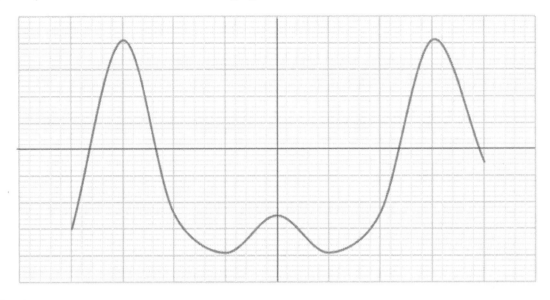

A. 1

B. 2

C. 3

D. 4

Answer: D

Explanation: The zeros of a function are the x-coordinate values when a function crosses the x axis. In the graph shown above, the function crosses the x-axis for a total of 4 times. Thus, the correct answer is D.

QUESTION 18

Select the answer choice that does NOT equal to the following rational expression:

$$\frac{m^2 + 9m + 18}{m^2 - m - 12}$$

A. $\dfrac{(m + 3) \times (m + 6)}{(m - 4) \times (m + 3)}$

B. $\dfrac{(m + 6)}{(m - 4)}$

C. $\dfrac{m^2 + 18 + 9m}{m^2 - 12 - m}$

D. $\left(\dfrac{m^2 + 9m + 18}{m^2 - m - 12}\right)^{-1}$

Answer: D

Explanation: To answer this question, it is necessary to factor the numerator and denominator, and then simplify the expression step by step. The numerator $(m^2 + 9m + 18)$ can be factored into $(m + 3)(m + 6)$. The denominator $(m^2 - m - 12)$ can be factored into $(m - 4)(m + 3)$.

Answer choice A is an expression equivalent to the original expression given because its numerator and denominator are simply factors of the numerator and denominator in the original expression.

Answer choice B is an expression equivalent to the original expression given because its numerator and denominator consists of the factors in the numerator and denominator in the original expression except for the $(m + 3)$, which has been removed since it appears in both the numerator and denominator.

Answer choice C is an expression equivalent to the original expression. The only change that has occurred is a rearrangement of the order in which the terms appear in the numerator and denominator, and this does not affect the value of the expression.

Answer choice D is an expression that is NOT equivalent to the original expression. The expression inside the parenthesis is equivalent to the expression originally given, but the expression in the parenthesis is raised to a -1 one exponent. This causes the entire expression inside to flip, which does not result in an equivalent form of the expression originally given.

QUESTION 19

Which of the following options is false?

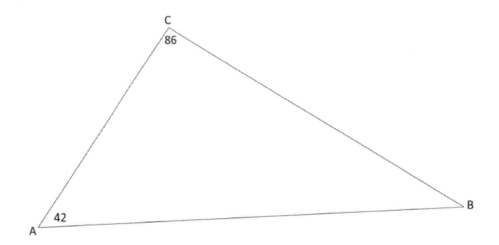

A. ∡CAB < ∡CBA < ∡BCA

B. $\overline{BC} < \overline{CA} < \overline{BA}$

C. ∡CAB + ∡CBA + ∡BCA = 180

D. $\overline{BA} > \overline{BC} > \overline{CA}$

Answer: D

Explanation: The best approach to this problem is to evaluate each option given

The first option requires knowledge of all three angles. Only two angles are given, so the third angle must be calculated. Knowing that the sum of three angles of a triangle adds to 180°, the known angles can be subtracted from 180°. This results in a value of 52° for the third angle. With three angles known, it becomes obvious that ∡CAB < ∡CBA < ∡BCA.

If the three angles are known, then the relative sizes of the three sides can be determined. The largest side of a triangle is opposite the largest angle of the triangle. The smallest side of a triangle is opposite the smallest angle of the triangle. With these two properties, it can be deduced that side BA is the largest and side BC is the smallest. This proves that option B is true.

As stated earlier, all three angles of a triangle sum to 180°, so this option is true.

Option D is false for the same reason that option B is true.

QUESTION 20

A chair manufacturer can build a maximum of 200 chairs in one month. The manufacturer takes orders of 5 chairs per order. For the month of March, the manufacturer has already secured orders for a total of 120 chairs. What is the maximum number of orders the manufacturer can add to the production for March?

    A. 16

    B. 40

    C. 80

    D. 120

Answer: A

Explanation: Since the manufacturer has secured orders for 120 chairs, the manufacturer can take orders for up to 80 more chairs as 200 – 120=80. With each order having 5 chairs, the number of orders the manufacture can take is 80 ÷ 5 =16.

QUESTION 21

Which number line below graphically represents the answer to the following inequality?

$$|4x + 12| < 2x + 12$$

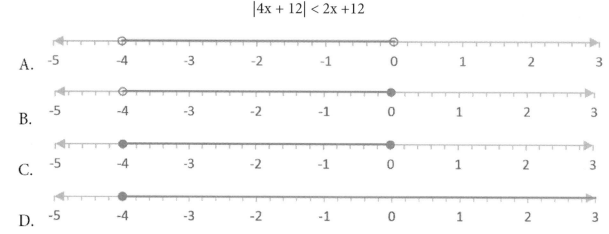

A.

B.

C.

D.

Answer: A

Explanation: To solve an inequality of the form $|x| < a$, the absolute value signs are removed and the following inequality is solved: $-a < x < a$. The left portion is solved: $-a < x$. The right portion is solved as $x < a$.

$|4x + 12| < 2x + 12$ becomes $-2x - 12 < 4x + 12 < 2x + 12$.

$4x + 12 < 2x + 12$ becomes $-2x - 12 + 12 - 4x < 4x + 12 + 12 - 4x$ which is equivalent to $-6x < 24$, resulting in $x > -4$

$4x + 12 < 2x + 12$ becomes $4x + 12 - 12 - 2x < 2x + 12 - 12 - 2x$ which is equivalent to $2x < 0$, resulting in $x < 0$

The answer to the inequality becomes $-4 < x < 0$. This inequality is depicted in the number line for answer A. Also, answer options B, C, and D can be discarded since they have closed dots at the end points. Closed dots represents symbols of $\leq$ and $\geq$.

QUESTION 22

Which of the following options is a median for the isosceles triangle shown below?

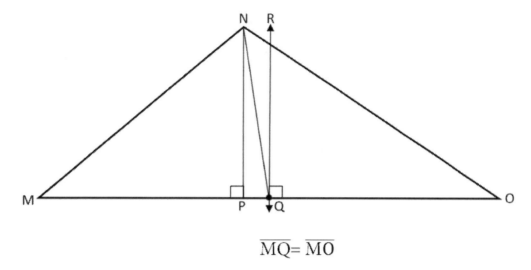

$$\overline{MQ} = \overline{MO}$$

A. $\overline{NP}$

B. $\overleftrightarrow{RQ}$

C. $\overline{NQ}$

D. $\overline{MQ}$

Answer: C

Explanation: The median is defined as the line segment that connects a vertex to the midpoint of the side opposite the vertex. In this figure, N is a vertex, and the midpoint on the opposite side is Q. The line segment $\overline{NQ}$ is a median from N to the middle of $\overline{MO}$.

QUESTION 23

Which of the following sets of numbers cannot be the measurements of the sides of a triangle?

    A. 6, 8, and 10

    B. 9, 12, and 22

    C. 7, 13, and 19

    D. 12, 19, and 25

Answer: B

Explanation: The sum of the shorter sides of the triangle has to be larger than the length of the hypotenuse.

QUESTION 24

John has been told by his parents that he can no longer spend more than $100 per month. In the first week of the month, John spent $14 on a movie ticket. In the second week, John spend $12 at the arcade. In the third week, John chose not to spend any money, so he could spend more the following week at his friend's birthday party. Which of the following number lines most accurately shows how much money John can spend in the last week of the month?

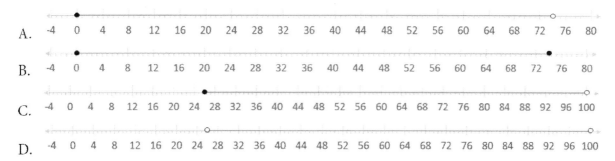

A. -4 0 4 8 12 16 20 24 28 32 36 40 44 48 52 56 60 64 68 72 76 80

B. -4 0 4 8 12 16 20 24 28 32 36 40 44 48 52 56 60 64 68 72 76 80

C. -4 0 4 8 12 16 20 24 28 32 36 40 44 48 52 56 60 64 68 72 76 80 84 88 92 96 100

D. -4 0 4 8 12 16 20 24 28 32 36 40 44 48 52 56 60 64 68 72 76 80 84 88 92 96 100

Answer: B

Explanation: Of the $100 restriction on his monthly expenditures, John has spent $14 the first week, $12 the second week, and $0 the third week. These three expenditures sum to a total value of $26, which results in $74 remaining in his total monthly budget. To ensure that John does not exceed his monthly restriction, John can spend anywhere between $0 and $74, as depicted in the number line shown in answer choice B.

Option B is chosen over Option A because Option B allows for John to spend $74, which would not exceed his budget. However, Option A only allows John to spent up $74 not $74.

QUESTION 25

A mechanic charges $50 an hour to fix a car and requires 65% reimbursement of any additional costs needed to fix the car. If the mechanic had to purchase $350 worth of the equipment to fix the car, how much of this cost will be paid back to the mechanic.

    A. $122.50

    B. $227.50

    C. $277.50

    D. $350.00

Answer: B

Explanation: The $350 spent represents additional costs needed to fix the car. The mechanic requires 65% of the costs to be reimbursed. 65% of the $350 is $227.50.

$$\frac{65}{100} \times 350 = 227.50$$

QUESTION 26

If $a < b < -1 < 0 < 1 < c < d$, then which of the following fractions has the smallest value?

A. $\dfrac{b}{a}$

B. $\dfrac{c}{d}$

C. $\dfrac{0}{c}$

D. $\dfrac{d}{b}$

Answer: D

Explanation: To solve this problem, the best approach is to analyze each option.

In option A, two negative numbers are being divided, so the result will be a positive number.

In option B, two positive numbers are being divided, so the result will be a positive number.

In option C, the numerator has a 0, so the result is 0.

In option D, a positive number is being divided by a negative number, so the result is a negative number.

Without knowing the magnitude of any of the values, it is certain option D will have the smallest value because it results in a negative number.

QUESTION 27

What digit will be in the hundreds place of 1.25468×10^{25}?

    A. 0

    B. 6

    C. 5

    D. 2

Answer: A

Explanation: In this problem, the number is represented in scientific notation. If the scientific notation was to be expanded to standard notation, the decimal place would move to the right 25 times. In front of the decimal, there will be 20 zeroes and the digits 125468. Since, the digit in the hundreds place is the value 3 units to the left of the decimal point; the hundred place for this number will be a zero.

QUESTION 28

In parallelogram MNOP, ∡M = x + 15 and ∡N = 3x + 5. What is the value of ∡P?

Answer: 125

Explanation: In a parallelogram, corresponding angles are supplementary and opposite angles are equivalent. Thus, ∡M and ∡N are supplementary and ∡N is equivalent to ∡P. The known information about angles M and N can be used to find the value of ∡N, which will be equivalent to ∡P.

The sum of angles M and N is equal to $4x + 20$, which is equivalent to 180. Solving for x yield a value of $x = 40$. Using this value of x in the definition of angle N yields a value of 125. Thus, angle P has a value of 125.

QUESTION 29

What is the result of performing this multiplication?

$$(-15 + 3i) \times (5 + 4i)$$

    A.   -87 – 45i

    B.   -87 – 33i

    C.   -63 – 45i

    D.   -63 – 33i

Answer: A

Explanation: The best approach is to first expand the multiplication out by multiplying each term with one another. The result of this is shown below. It is important to note that $i \times i = -1$. After multiplying each term, the results are simplified, also shown below.

$$-15 \times 5 + -15 \times 4i + 3i \times 5 + 3i \times 4i = -75 + -60i + 15i -12 = -87 – 45i$$

QUESTION 30

What value(s) of x will satisfy the following equation?

$$18x^2 + 24x + 8 = 0$$

A. 0

B. -2/3

C. 2/3

D. 2/3 and -2/3

Answer: B

Explanation: The best approach to this problem is to use the quadratic formula, which is shown below. In the quadratic formula, the variables a, b, and c correspond to the standard form of a quadratic equation: $ax^2 + bx + c = 0$. In this problem a = 18, b = 24, and c = 8. When these values are inserted into the quadratic formula, x = -2/3.

$$x = \frac{-b \pm \sqrt{b^2 - 4ac}}{2a}$$

$$x = \frac{-24 \pm \sqrt{24^2 - 4 \times 18 \times 8}}{2 \times 18}$$

$$x = \frac{-24 \pm \sqrt{0}}{2 \times 18}$$

$$x = \frac{-24}{36} = -\frac{2}{3}$$

QUESTION 31

John's weekly income consists of his hourly wages and a $50 weekly allowance given to him by his father. Maria's weekly income consists of her hourly wages and a weekly allowance given to her by her father. John earns $10 an hour and Maria earns $12 an hour. If they each work for 10 hours in one week, how much weekly allowance does Maria's father need to give her, so both Maria and John earn the same income in that week?

    A. $20

    B. $30

    C. $50

    D. $120

Answer: B

Explanation: To solve this problem, John's weekly income needs to be calculated. He earns $50 from his father and $100 from his work (10 hours × $10/hr); this adds to a total weekly income of $150. The next step is to model Maria's income as a function of her allowance and hours worked. This model is a linear equation equal to $12h + b$; where h is the hours worked and b is her allowance. Since the problem states Maria's income should be equal to John's income, the linear equation is set equal to $150. The problems also states she works for 10 hours, so h will equal to 10 in the equation. These two substitutions result in $12 \times 10 + b = 150$, which can be solved for b = $30.

QUESTION 32

Solve for x and y:

$$12x + 12y = 40$$
$$8x + 4y = 32$$

A. $x = -11\frac{1}{3}$ and $y = 14\frac{2}{3}$

B. $x = -1\frac{5}{9}$ and $y = 4\frac{8}{9}$

C. $x = 4\frac{2}{3}$ and $y = -8\frac{1}{3}$

D. $x = 4\frac{2}{3}$ and $y = -1\frac{1}{3}$

Answer: D

Explanation: The best approach is to multiply the second equation by 3. This will allow the two equations to be subtracted, and the y variable to disappear. After multiplying the second equation by 3, the equation becomes $24x + 12y = 96$. When the second equation is subtracted from the first equation, the difference is $-12x = -56$; this results in an x value of $4\frac{2}{3}$. Substituting this value for x into any of the two equations can allow solving for y. Substituting $4\frac{2}{3}$ into the first equation results in a y-value of $-1\frac{1}{3}$. The same y value will result if the x value is substituted into the second equation.

QUESTION 33

The graph below represents the solution to which of the following inequalities

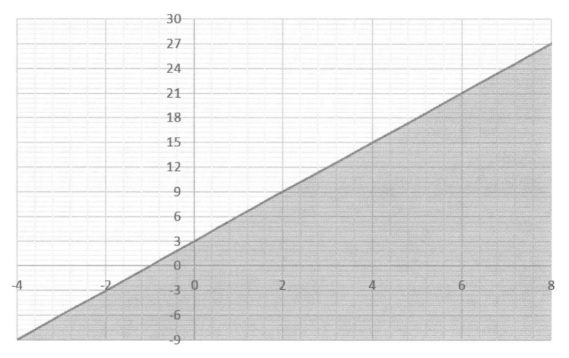

A. y < -3x – 3

B. y ≤ 3x + 3

C. y < 3x + 3

D. y ≥ 3x + 3

Answer: B

Explanation: The line indicates a linear equation defined as y= 3x + 3. The solid line indicates that values on the line are solutions to the inequality. The shading below the line indicates all values that are less than the values defined on the line are also solutions to the inequality. These descriptions are matched with the inequality shown in answer choice B.

QUESTION 34

What are the next three numbers in the following sequence?

10, 40, 160, 640

    A. 2560, 10240, 40960

    B. 10240, 40960, 163840,

    C. 10, 40, 160

    D. 640, 2560, 10240

Answer: A

Explanation: In the sequence, each next number is equivalent to the previous number multiplied by 4.

QUESTION 35

Given f(x) = 5x + 20 and g(x) = 6x + 12, what is f(g(3))?

    A. 30

    B. 35

    C. 170

    D. 222

Answer: C

Explanation: The first step is to calculate the value of g(3); this is obtained by substituting 3 for the value of x in g(x) = 6x + 12. After this substitution, g(3) = 30. Next, the value of x in f(x) = 5x + 20 must substituted with the value of g(3), which is 30. This substitution will result in 170, which is the answer.

QUESTION 36

In his algebra class, John's professor assigns 3 group projects and 3 exams. The three group projects are worth 20%, 25%, and 20%, respectively, of the final course grade. The three exams are worth 10%, 15%, and 10% of the final course grade. If John earned a 73, 75, and 97 on the group projects, respectively, and a 99, 93, and 100 on the exams, respectively, then what is his final course grade?

    A. 91.3

    B. 89.5

    C. 86.6

    D. 78.2

Answer: C

Explanation: This problem requires the weighted average to be taken. There are 6 data values that contribute to the final course grade, and each value contributes to the final course grade differently. The 99 on the first exam has a 10% value to the final course grade, so it contributes a value of 9.9. The 93 on the second exam has a 15% value to the final course grade, so it contributes a value of 13.95. The 100 on the third exam has a 10% value to the final course grade, so it contributes a value of 10. The 73 on the first project has a value of 20% to the final course grade, so it contributes a value of 14.6. The 75 on the second project has a value of 25% to the final course grade, so it contributes a value of 18.75. The 97 on the third project has a value of 20% to the final course grade, so it contributes a value of 19.4. The 6 data values contribute a total of 9.9 + 13.95 + 10 + 14.6 + 18.75 + 19.4=86.6 to the final course grade. Since these 6 data values are the contributors to the final course grade, the final grade will be 86.6.

QUESTION 37

The owner of a local gym asked people in the community how many hours they work out during the week. The owner recorded his results in the line plot below. What is the median, mode, and range of the data set?

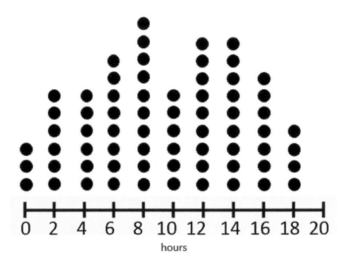

A. Median = 8; Mode = 10; Range =20

B. Median = 9; Mode = 8; Range = 18

C. Median = 10; Mode = 8; Range = 1

D. Median = 16; Mode = 10; Range = 16

Answer: B

Explanation: The mode of the data set will be 8 because 8 hours has the most values associated with it. The range of the data set will be 18 because 18 hours is the largest recorded value and 0 hours is the smallest recorded data value. The median of the data set will be 9 because the two central numbers in the data set are 8 hours and 10 hours.

QUESTION 38

What of the following scenarios can be modeled by the line graph shown below?

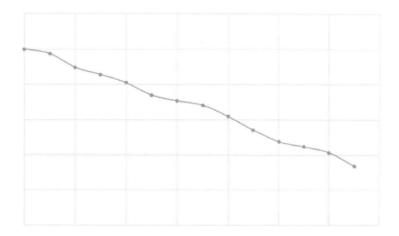

A. At the end of every year, Marcus takes his car to the dealership. The mechanic at the dealership performs the annual check-ups and tells Marcus the market value of the car. Marcus takes the value of the car at the end of each year and creates a line graph.

B. Michael takes out a loan from a bank. He pays off equal portions of the loan every month. Michael wants to create a line graph that shows the value of loan he had remaining at the end of each month that he made a payment in.

C. Maria takes out a loan from a bank. She pays off equal portions of the loan every month. Maria wants to create a line graph that shows the cumulative sum of money she has given to the bank at the end of each month.

D. A and B

Answer: A

Explanation: The line graph shown displays decreasing values of a variable with respect to increasing time. This is enough reasoning to prevent the line graph to model the situation in option C; the situation in option C has increasing values as time increases.

Furthermore, the amount of decrease with respect to time is not constant, which explains the lack of a linear relationship among the data points. Since the variable does not change constantly, option B cannot be modeled with the line graph shown. The situation in option B indicates that equal portions are paid every month, which would imply a constant change with respect to time.

Option A is the correct answer. The value of the car would decrease with respect time, and the change in the value cannot be guaranteed to be equal every year.

QUESTION 39

The following pie chart breaks down several of the expenses for a grocery store in a given year. If a total of $923,800 was spent on wages, how much money was spent on taxes and physical capital?

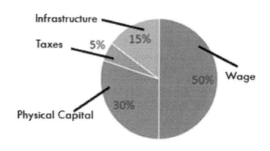

A. $1,847,600

B. $646,660

C. $554,280

D. $92,380

Answer: B

Explanation: The pie chart shows that wages take up 50% of the total expenses for the four categories. To find the total expenses for the four expense categories, the following ratio is used. The variable x represents the total expenses for the four categories.

$$\frac{1}{2} = \frac{\$923,800}{X}$$

The ratio above yields an x-value of $1,847,600. This amount of money represents the total amount of expenses for the four categories shown. The problem statement asks for the total expenses for taxes and physical capital. These two categories represent 35% of the total amount of expenses for the four categories. Thus, the total money spent on taxes and physical capital will be $1,847,600 × 0.35=$646,660.

QUESTION 40

Marissa's neighbors have 3 dogs. What is the probability that two of the three dogs are male?

    A. 0.875

    B. 0.500

    C. 0.375

    D. 0.250

Answer: D

Explanation: The best approach to this problem is to first list all the possible outcomes of the gender of the three dogs. This will represent the sample space. These outcomes are:

        FFF   FFM   FMF   MFF   MMM MMF MFM FMM

Of the sample space, only 3 of the 8 outcomes have two dogs as male, so the probably that two of the three dogs are male is 0.375.

This page is intentionally left blank.

Constructed Response 1

Use the data provided to complete the task that follows.

Using the data provided, prepare a response of approximately 400–600 words in which you:

- identify an important mathematical strength related to the standard that is demonstrated by the student, citing specific evidence from the exhibits to support your assessment;
- identify an important area of need related to the standard that is demonstrated by the student, citing specific evidence from the exhibits to support your assessment; and
- describe an instructional plan that builds on the student's strengths and that would help the student improve in the identified area of need. Include a plan for assisting the student build a viable argument related to the given standard.

Eighth-grade students have been developing their understanding functions and modeling relationships between quantities. The class is currently working on the following standard from the New York State P–12 Common Core Learning Standards for Mathematics:

CCSS.Math.Content.8.F.B.4

Construct a function to model a linear relationship between two quantities. Determine the rate of change and initial value of the function from a description of a relationship or from two (x, y) values, including reading these from a table or from a graph. Interpret the rate of change and initial value of a linear function in terms of the situation it models, and in terms of its graph or a table of values.

Description of Class Activity

The teacher pairs students and has the students complete the following activity:

A company is going to buy new manufacturing units. Brand A costs $250,000 to buy and $10,000 a month to operate. Brand B costs $450,000 to buy, but only cost $4,000 a month to operate.

Use a system of linear equations to analyze the cost of purchasing and operating each of these two brands. Your response should show all work and include:

F. a particular equation for each unit expressing the total cost of operation as a function of the number of months since the purchase of the unit;

G. a sketch of the graphs of the two equations on one set of coordinate axes, with the axes, scales, intercepts, and any calculated points clearly labeled;

H. an explanation of the slope and intercepts of each function in the context of the problem situation;

I. calculation of the "break-even" point for the two functions, i.e., the number of months for which the total cost of the two units would be the same; and

J. advice for the company as to which would be the less expensive option.

Excerpt of Student's Work
Part B

Both equations are linear, so just two points are needed per graph. For Brand A, choose the initial point when t=0, and a point down the line, let's say t=100 months. The data points for Brand A are shown in the table below.

Time (months)	Work	Total Cost ($)
0	Brand A = $10,000(0) + $250,000	250,000
100	Brand A = $10,000(100) + $250,000	1,250,000

Similarly for Brand B, the data points are shown in the table below.

Time (months)	Work	Total Cost ($)
0	Brand B = $4,000(0) + $450,000	450,000
100	Brand B = $4,000(100) + $450,000	850,000

Sketch both lines in the same graph by connecting the points.

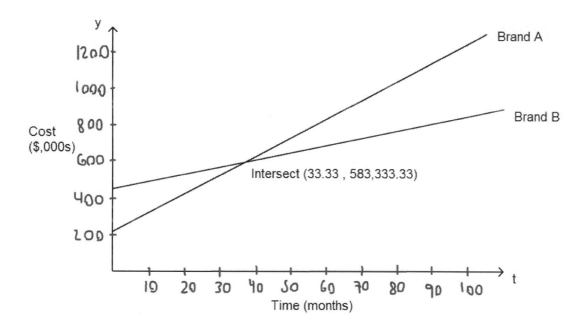

Excerpt of Conversation With Teacher

Teacher: What did you used to graph the lines?

Student: I used the information in the question to draw the graph.

Teacher: What specifically did you used to draw the lines?

Student: Brand A cost $250,000, so when it is 0 months that will be the value on the y-axis.

Teacher: Is that the y-intercept?

Student: Yes

Teacher: What else did you used?

Student: Brand B cost $450,000, so when it is 0 months that will be the value on the y-axis.

Teacher: Anything else you used to graph the lines?

Student: There is increase of $10,000 for Brand A and $4,000 for Brand B, so I just increased roughly that amount each month.

Teacher: Can you tell me the slope values for these equations?

Student: The slope is going to be the x-intercept values.

NOTE: Note: To receive individualized feedback, email essay to onlinepreparationservices@gmail.com and allow 5-7 days for feedback.

Practice Test 2

This page is intentionally left blank.

Exam Answer Sheet – Test 2

Below is an optional answer sheet to use to document answers.

Question Number	Selected Answer	Question Number	Selected Answer
1		21	
2		22	
3		23	
4		24	
5		25	
6		26	
7		27	
8		28	
9		29	
10		30	
11		31	
12		32	
13		33	
14		34	
15		35	
16		36	
17		37	
18		38	
19		39	
20		40	

This page is intentionally left blank.

QUESTION 1

Which of the following is equivalent to $2^x + 12^x$?

    A. 14^x

    B. 24^x

    C. $2^x(1 + 6^x)$

    D. 3×4^x

Answer:

QUESTION 2

Every month, a telephone company charges $0.10 for each minute of telephone usage in that month. If a customer exceeds the limit of 700 minutes per month, then for every additional minute, the charge per minute increases to $0.15. Which expression below is equal to the monthly telephone usage charge, expressed as variable c, for a customer who used the telephone for 24 hours in one month?

    A. $c = 700 \times \$0.15 + 740 \times \$0.10$

    B. $c = 1440 \times \$0.15$

    C. $c = 1440 \times \$0.10$

    D. $c = 700 \times 0.10 + 740 \times \$0.15$

Answer:

QUESTION 3

In Edward's class, there are 12 boys for every 20 girls. What percent of the total class are girls?

    A. 62.5%

    B. 60%

    C. 80%

    D. 85%

Answer:

QUESTION 4

What equation represents the graph shown below?

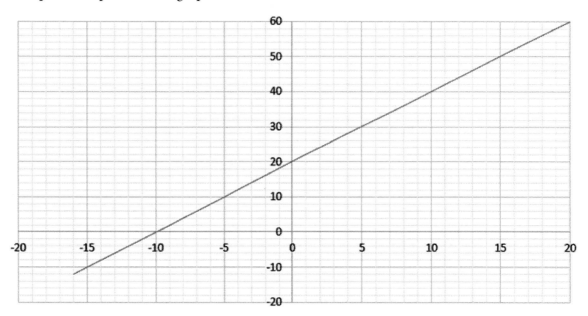

A. y = x + 20

B. y = -2x

C. y = 2x + 20

D. y = 2x - 20

Answer:

QUESTION 5

Which of the following equations will NOT produce the graph shown below?

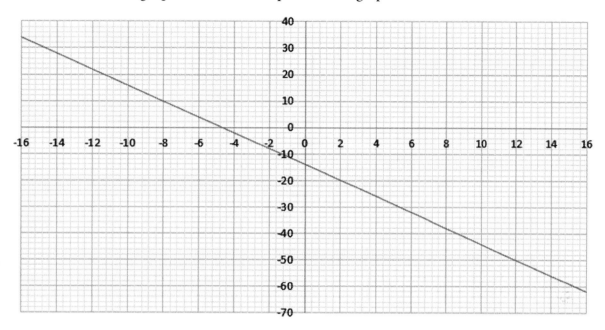

A. y = -3x – 14

B. y = - (3x + 14)

C. y – 4 = -3 (x + 6)

D. y – 20 = -3 (x + 2)

Answer:

QUESTION 6

What is the solution to the following set of operations?

$$\left(\frac{5}{4}\right)^{-2} \times 5^3 \times \frac{\sqrt{18 \times 2 + 3 \times 2^2}}{80}$$

A. $4\sqrt{3}$

B. $3\sqrt{3}$

C. $3\sqrt{4}$

D. $4\sqrt{16}$

Answer:

QUESTION 7

Joanna wants to enlarge the rectangular poster on her wall. She wants to enlarge the poster so it can have an area of 256 in^2, but wants the ratio of the height to the width to remain 1:4. What should the width of the enlarged poster be?

    A. 8

    B. 16

    C. 32

    D. Not enough information given to solve the problem

Answer:

QUESTION 8

After a test, an instructor asked 5 students in the class how many hours they studied for the test. The students' responses are listed in the table below along with their test scores. What function, if any, describes the relationship between the hours studied and the score obtained by the students?

Student	Hours Studied	Exam Score
1	15	70
2	20	80
3	3	46
4	1	42
5	30	100

    A. $e(h) = h^2 - 120$

    B. $e(h) = 3h + 20$

    C. $e(h) = 2h + 40$

    D. None of the above

Answer:

QUESTION 9

If Y is the dependent variable in the tables below, which of the following tables contains values that does not defines a function?

A

X	Y
5	123
8	510
12	1726
18	5830
23	12165

B

X	Y
-10	15
-5	10
0	5
5	10
10	15

C

X	Y
-10	913
-8	457
0	-7
16	-4391
24	-14455

D

X	Y
12	114
20	210
30	330
37	414
37	444

Answer:

QUESTION 10

What value(s) of x are NOT included in the domain of this function?

$$f(x) = \frac{x^2 + 5x - 14}{x^2 - 7x + 10}$$

A. x = −2, x = −5

B. x = 7

C. x = −5

D. x = 2, x = 5, and x = −7

Answer:

QUESTION 11

A cable connects the top of a post with the ground as shown in the figure below. The distance between the base of the tower and the base of the cable is 36 feet, and the cable has an angle of elevation of 35° with respect to the ground.

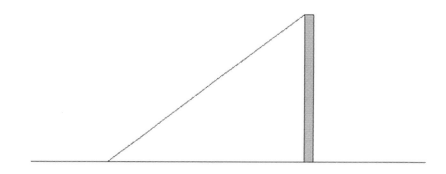

Note: Figure not drawn to scale.

What is the approximate height in feet of the post?

A. 17

B. 20

C. 22

D. 25

Answer:

QUESTION 12

Which of the following functions cannot be classified as an even function?

    A. $|x| + 3 = f(x)$

    B. $x^2 + 3 = f(x)$

    C. $x^4 + 3 = f(x)$

    D. $x + 3 = f(x)$

Answer:

QUESTION 13

Given that points I, J, and K represent the midpoints for their respective sides on $\triangle ABC$, what is the perimeter of triangle ABC?

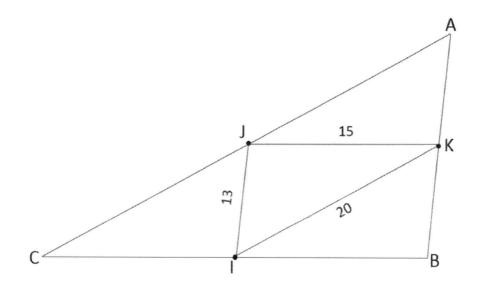

    A. 48

    B. 72

    C. 96

    D. 108

Answer:

QUESTION 14

In parallelogram ABCD (not shown), ∢B = x + 15 and ∢C = 3x + 5. Which of the following statements regarding the diagonals of the parallelogram is true?

    A. $\overline{BD} = \overline{CA}$

    B. $\overline{BD} < \overline{CA}$

    C. $\overline{BD} > \overline{CA}$

    D. Not enough information given

Answer:

QUESTION 15

Which of the following statements accurately describes a rhombus?

    A. The diagonals of the quadrilateral are perpendicular

    B. The diagonals of the quadrilateral are congruent

    C. The diagonals of the quadrilateral bisect one another

    D. A and C

Answer:

QUESTION 16

Which of the following line segment(s) represents a chord on the circle shown below?

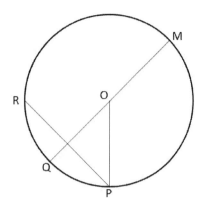

A. $\overline{RP}$

B. $\overline{PO}$

C. $\overline{MQ}$

D. A and C

Answer:

QUESTION 17

Which of the following scatter plots shows that there may be some degree of correlation between the dependent and independent variables?

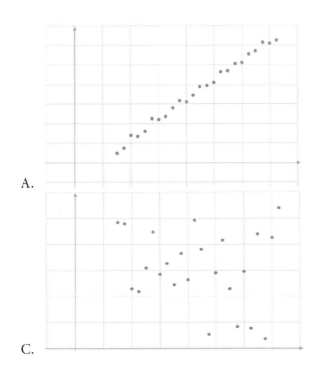
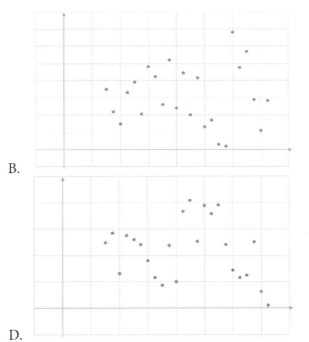

A.

B.

C.

D.

Answer:

QUESTION 18

When a six sided standard die is tossed once, what is the probability of getting 1, 3, and a 9?

    A. $\frac{1}{6}$

    B. $\frac{3}{6}$

    C. 0

    D. Undefined

Answer:

QUESTION 19

Sets A and B are defined below. Which of the following sets represents A∩ B?

$$A = \{3, 6, 9, 12, 15, 18\}$$

$$B = \{2, 4, 6, 8, 10, 12, 14\}$$

   A. {2, 3, 4, 6, 8, 9, 10, 12, 14, 15, 18}

   B. 2, 3, 4, 6, 8, 9, 10, 12, 14, 15, 18

   C. {6, 12}

   D. A and B

Answer:

QUESTION 20

A set has the following 10 numbers: 12, 19, 25, 28, 54, 26, 87, 23, 98, and 25. If an 11th number is to be added to the set, what does the number have to be in order for the set to have a mean of 40?

   A. -43

   B. 3

   C. 40

   D. 43

Answer:

QUESTION 21

A data set with a mean of 75 and a standard deviation of 3.5 is known to have a normal distribution. What percent of the data does NOT lie between 71.5 and 78.5?

    A. 99.95

    B. 68.2

    C. 31.8

    D. not enough information given

Answer:

QUESTION 22

Which of the following ratios is not equal to 68%?

    A. 68:100

    B. 34:50

    C. 102:150

    D. 17:50

Answer:

QUESTION 23

Solve the following problem:

$$(5-1\times0+3\div3)\times\left(5+3\times2^{4}\right)\times\left(\frac{21\times3\times\frac{1}{7}}{5-1\times4\times3+2}\right)$$

    A. 0

    B. -572.4

    C. -230.4

    D. 57.24

Answer:

QUESTION 24

Chris' family drove a distance of 300 miles in 2 hours. Pat's family drove a distance of 400 miles in 3 hours. What is the ratio of the speed of Chris' family to the speed of Pat's family?

 A. 9/8

 B. 8/9

 C. 3/4

 D. 2/3

Answer:

QUESTION 25

Which of the following represents the Commutative Property of Multiplication?

 A. $a \times b \times c = a \times b^c$

 B. $a \times b \times c = b \times c \times a$

 C. $a \times b \times c = a \times b \times c$

 D. $a \times b \times c = a + b + c$

Answer:

QUESTION 26

What are the values for the domain in the graph shown below?

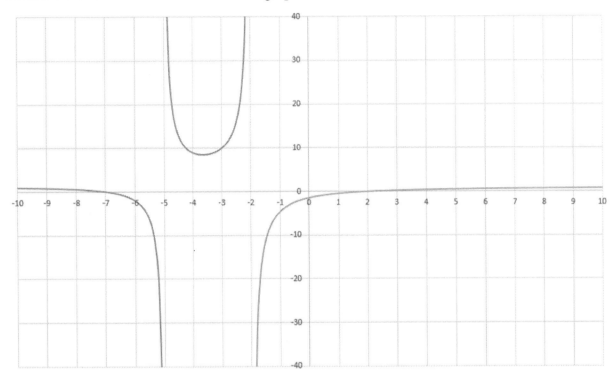

A. [−5, −2]

B. [−∞,−5) U (−5, −2) U (−2, ∞]

C. (−∞,−5) U [−5, −2] U (−2, ∞)

D. None of the above

Answer:

QUESTION 27

Which of the following is NOT equivalent to the radical below?

$$\sqrt[3]{324}$$

    A. $3 \times \sqrt[3]{12}$

    B. $\left(\frac{1}{324}\right)^{-\frac{1}{3}}$

    C. $\left((324)^2\right)^{\frac{1}{6}}$

    D. 18

Answer:

QUESTION 28

Of the following equations, which equation has an x – intercept greater than the y – intercept and a slope equal to the absolute value of the y – intercept.

    A. $y = 2x - 2$

    B. $y = 4x - 16$

    C. $y = 0.5x - 0.5$

    D. A and C

Answer:

QUESTION 29

What would be the y-intercept of the graph?

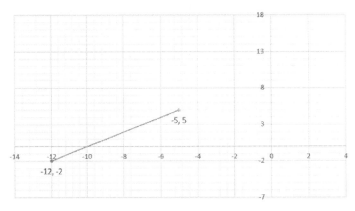

A. 13

B. 10

C. -14

D. -10

Answer:

QUESTION 30

The table below shows the length of time in minutes 25 drivers were stuck in traffic during rush hour. Which of the following values cannot be determined from the data set shown below?

Time	Number of Drivers
0.0-5.5	3
5.5-15.5	10
15.5-25.5	8
25.5-30.5	1
30.5-45.5	3

A. range

B. mean

C. median

D. cannot be answered

Answer:

QUESTION 31

A new ice cream store has opened, and the owner of the store has surveyed the first 100 customers. The survey showed that 67 customers have tried their homemade chocolate flavor and 82 customers have tried their homemade vanilla flavor. Of the 100 customers surveyed, 27 customers have tried the homemade vanilla flavor but not the homemade chocolate flavor. How many customers have tried neither the homemade vanilla flavor nor the homemade chocolate flavor?

    A. 6

    B. 12

    C. 40

    D. 55

Answer:

QUESTION 32

Mark and his wife are at the grand opening of a car dealership because they each want to win the two prizes that are being raffled away. Every attendee at the grand opening is allowed to write one name on a slip of paper and place that paper into a jar. Each attendee can get one prize. The manager will then select one name from the jar, and this person will have the option of choosing his or her prize. The manger will then select another name from the jar, and this person will take the remaining prize. If Mark and his wife have counted a total of 320 slips in the jar, what is the probability that they will each go home with a prize.

    A. 9.80×10^{-6}

    B. 6.25×10^{-3}

    C. 9.77×10^{-6}

    D. 1.96×10^{-5}

Answer:

QUESTION 33

Which of the following events are mutually exclusive?

    A. The event of a getting an odd number and an even number when a single card is drawn from a deck.

    B. The event of getting a 3 and an odd number when a die is tossed.

    C. The event of getting 7 and a number less than 9 when a single card is drawn from a deck.

    D. The event of getting a 5 and a number less than 6 when a die is tossed.

Answer:

QUESTION 34

On a school field trip, Timothy has to choose a walking buddy to accompany him to the vending machine. Of the thirty students he can choose from, 20 are older than him and 10 are younger than him. Of the 20 students older than Timothy, 12 are boys, and of the 10 students younger than him, 6 are girls. What is the probability that Timothy chooses a walking buddy that is older than him or a boy?

    A. $\dfrac{6}{5}$

    B. $\dfrac{2}{3}$

    C. $\dfrac{4}{5}$

    D. $\dfrac{11}{15}$

Answer:

QUESTION 35

Which of the following situations describes dependent events?

    A. The probability of selecting a quarter from a piggy bank and then selecting a penny.

    B. The probability of getting 3 from a single toss of a die and then another 3 from another toss of the die.

    C. The probability of selecting a quarter from a piggy bank and then selecting a penny after the quarter has been put back.

    D. A and C

Answer:

QUESTION 36

A shoe store receives a weekly shipment of 100 shoes on Sunday night, so that it can have full inventory to sell from on Monday morning. In a certain week, the store manager was notified that the shipment for that week contained 5 shoes that were damaged due to mishandling. If this notification came Tuesday, and 5 of the 100 delivered shoes were sold the previous day (Monday), what is the probability that at least 1 of the 5 shoes sold was damaged?

    A. 0.05

    B. 0.230

    C. 0.770

    D. 0.95

Answer:

QUESTION 37

Coach Johnson tells his quarterback to stand 50 yards away from the poster shown below, and throw the football at the shaded circle. The intention of this drill is to improve the accuracy of the quarterback's throws. If the quarterback's throw hits the poster, what is the probability that it will hit the shaded circle?

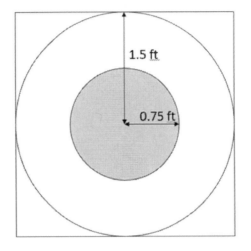

A. 0.196

B. 0.250

C. 0.520

D. 0.785

Answer:

QUESTION 38

Of the equations below, which equation does NOT have an x–intercept of 5 and a y–intercept of 15?

    A. $y = -3x + 15$

    B. $y + 15 = -2 \times (x - 15)$

    C. $2y = -6x + 30$

    D. $y - 9 = -3 \times (x - 2)$

Answer:

QUESTION 39

Which of the following line(s) represents an axis of symmetry for $y = 6x^2 + 24x - 24$?

    A. $x = -2$

    B. $x = -2$ and $y = -24$

    C. $x = 2$

    D. $x = 0$

Answer:

QUESTION 40

Which of the following expressions is equivalent to the expression below?

$$\left(\frac{6-x}{5x-30}\right)^{-1} \times \left(\frac{5yx+5y}{10yx+5yx}\right)$$

    A. $\dfrac{(x+1)}{15x}$

    B. $\dfrac{-5y(x+6)}{3x}$

    C. $\dfrac{-5(x+1)}{3x}$

    D. $\dfrac{3(x+1)}{5}$

Answer:

Constructed Response 1

Use the data provided to complete the task that follows.

Using the data provided, prepare a response of approximately 400–600 words in which you:

- identify an important mathematical strength related to the standard that is demonstrated by the student, citing specific evidence from the exhibits to support your assessment;
- identify an important area of need related to the standard that is demonstrated by the student, citing specific evidence from the exhibits to support your assessment; and
- describe an instructional plan that builds on the student's strengths and that would help the student improve in the identified area of need. Include a plan for assisting the student build a viable argument related to the given standard.

Eighth-grade students have been developing their understanding functions and modeling relationships between quantities. The class is currently working on the following standard from the New York State P–12 Common Core Learning Standards for Mathematics:

CCSS.Math.Content.8.F.A.3

Interpret the equation $y = mx + b$ as defining a linear function, whose graph is a straight line; give examples of functions that are not linear.

Description of Class Activity

A father is considering two options to give an allowance at the end of each month to his teenage son for 12 months, provided the son completes all his house chores. The two options are:

Option 1: Receive $20 at the end of the first month. Every month thereafter receive 15% more than the previous month.

Option 2: Receive $50 at the end of the first month. Every month thereafter receive $1 more than the allowance of the previous month.

Use your knowledge of exponential and linear functions to develop a response in which you analyze the allowance received each month during a 12-month period under each option. In your response:

A. create a data table representing the allowance received each month over a 12-month period for each option;
B. graph the data from both tables on the same coordinate grid and connect the data with the line or curve that best fits the data;
C. compare the allowance plans over the 12-month period, including a discussion of the significance of the point of intersection of the two graphs;
D. explain what type of function, exponential or linear, models each option;
E. find equations that describe each option; and
F. identify an expression that represents the difference between the allowances received under the two options in the twelfth month.

Be sure to show your work and explain the reasoning you use in analyzing and solving this problem.

Excerpt of Student's Work

Part A

The tables representing the allowances received each month over the 12-month period for the two options are shown below.

Option 1

Month	1	2	3	4	5	6	7	8	9	10	11	12
Allowance ($)	20	23	26.45	30.42	34.98	40.23	46.26	53.2	61.18	70.36	80.91	93.05

Each new value is obtained by taking the previous month and adding the 15% of the previous month. This is shown below.

$$\text{New Value} = \text{Previous Month Value} + 15\% \text{ of Previous Month Value}$$

For the second month, the calculation is shown next.

$$\text{New Value} = 20 + 0.15(20) = 20 + 3 = 23$$

Other values are obtained similarly.

Option 2

Month	1	2	3	4	5	6	7	8	9	10	11	12
Allowance ($)	50	51	52	53	54	55	56	57	58	59	60	61

Part D

Option 1 shows a curve that is linear up until month 9, where it starts to become steeper as time goes by. Therefore, it is an exponential function.

Option 2 shows a constant increase of $1. Therefore, it is a linear function.

Excerpt of Conversation With Teacher

Teacher: How did you find the equation for Option 1?

Student: I used the standard slope formula.

Teacher: What is that formula?

Student: $y=mx+b$

Teacher: Why did you use this formula?

Student: Because there is almost a constant change, so that is the best way to write equation.

Teacher: How did you use this formula to write the equation?

Student: I took two points. I used two points to find the slope. Then, used the slope and one coordinate to find the formula.

Teacher: Is there any other way that you can find the equation?

Student: I don't think so.

Middle School Practice Exam Answers – Test 2

Question Number	Selected Answer	Question Number	Selected Answer
1	C	21	C
2	D	22	D
3	A	23	B
4	C	24	A
5	D	25	B
6	A	26	D
7	C	27	D
8	C	28	D
9	D	29	B
10	A	30	D
11	D	31	A
12	D	32	D
13	C	33	A
14	C	34	C
15	D	35	A
16	D	36	B
17	A	37	A
18	C	38	B
19	C	39	A
20	D	40	C

NOTE: Getting approximately 80% of the questions correct increases chances of obtaining passing score on the real exam. This varies from different states and university programs.

This page is intentionally left blank.

QUESTION 1

Which of the following is equivalent to $2^x + 12^x$?

    A. 14^x

    B. 24^x

    C. $2^x (1 + 6^x)$

    D. 3×4^x

Answer: C

Explanation: It is important to note that $12^x = (2 \times 6)^x = 2^x \times 6^x$. With this equivalency, an expression of $2^x + 2^x \times 6^x$ can be factored. The common factor in both terms of the addition is 2^x. When this factor is taken out of the expression the result is $2^x (1 + 6^x)$.

QUESTION 2

Every month, a telephone company charges $0.10 for each minute of telephone usage in that month. If a customer exceeds the limit of 700 minutes per month, then for every additional minute, the charge per minute increases to $0.15. Which expression below is equal to the monthly telephone usage charge, expressed as variable c, for a customer who used the telephone for 24 hours in one month?

    A. c = 700×$0.15 + 740×$0.10

    B. c = 1440×$0.15

    C. c = 1440×$0.10

    D. c = 700×0.10 + 740×$0.15

Answer: D

Explanation: The telephone usage charge can consists of two separate expenditures. The first expenditure will be the cost for using the telephone for up to 700 minutes. The second expenditure, which may or may not exist, is for using the telephone for any minutes in excess of 700 minutes. In this problem, it is stated that the total usage is 24 hours, which is equivalent to 24 × 60 = 1440 minutes. Since 1440 minutes is greater than 700 minutes, the second expenditure will exist. The first expenditure will be the cost of the first 700 minutes used, which can be expressed by 700 × $0.10. The second expenditure will be for the cost of the 740 minutes in excess of the 1440 – 700=740 minutes, which can be expressed as 740×$0.15. The total cost is the sum of the two expenditures and is expressed by answer choice D.

QUESTION 3

In Edward's class, there are 12 boys for every 20 girls. What percent of the total class are girls?

    A. 62.5%

    B. 60%

    C. 80%

    D. 85%

Answer: A

Explanation: If there are 12 boys for every 20 girls in the class, then, for a total of 32 students, there will be 20 girls. 20 girls for every 32 students represents a percentage of $\left(\frac{20}{32}\right) \times 100\% = 62.5\%$.

QUESTION 4

What equation represents the graph shown below?

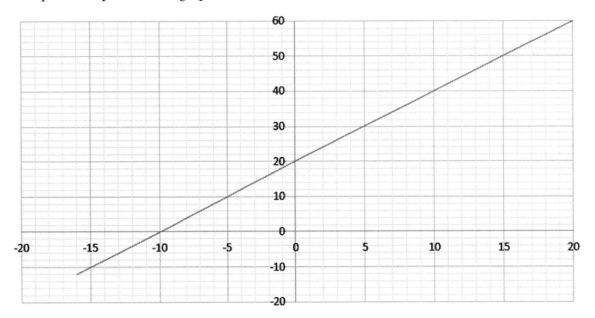

A. y = x + 20

B. y = -2x

C. y = 2x + 20

D. y = 2x - 20

Answer: C

Explanation: Each of the answer choices given above are in the standard form of a linear equation: y = mx + b; where m is the slope and b is the y-intercept. The graph shown above has a y-intercept of 20. The slope can be calculated by choosing two points and using the slope formula, which is shown below. The two points chosen can be (0, 20) and (10, 40); these two points result in a slope of 2. Thus, the linear equation is: y = 2x + 20.

$$m = \frac{y_2 - y_1}{x_2 - x_1}$$

$$m = \frac{40-20}{10-0} = 2$$

QUESTION 5

Which of the following equations will NOT produce the graph shown below?

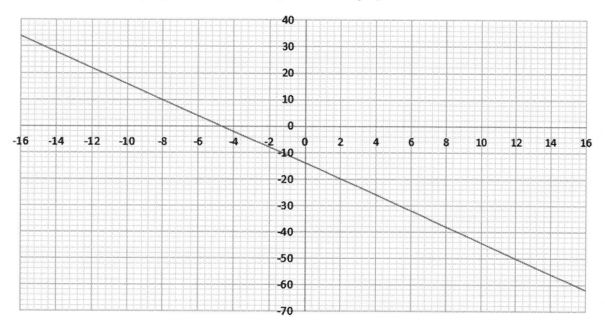

A. $y = -3x - 14$

B. $y = -(3x + 14)$

C. $y - 4 = -3(x + 6)$

D. $y - 20 = -3(x + 2)$

Answer: D

Explanation: The answer choices are the linear equations in two different formats: the point-slope formula and the standard formula.

The standard formula is expressed as $y = mx + b$; where m is the slope and b is the y intercept. In this graph, the y – intercept can be read as -14. The slope can be calculated from the slope formula, which is shown below. Two points are necessary to calculate the slope; these two points are chosen to be (2, -20) and (4, -26). The points result in a slope of -3. Thus, the equation of the graph in standard linear form is $y = -3x - 14$. This is also equivalent to $y = -(3x + 14)$.

$$m = \frac{y_2 - y_1}{x_2 - x_1}$$

$$m = \frac{-26 - (-20)}{4 - 2} = -3$$

The point slope formula is expressed as $y - y_1 = m (x - x_1)$; where m is the slope and (x_1, y_1) is a point on the line. In answer choice C, the point is taken to be (-6, 4), which is a point on the line. However, in answer choice D, the point is taken to be (-2, 20), which is not on the line. Thus, the correct answer for this problem is D.

QUESTION 6

What is the solution to the following set of operations?

$$\left(\frac{5}{4}\right)^{-2} \times 5^3 \times \frac{\sqrt{18 \times 2 + 3 \times 2^2}}{80}$$

A. $4\sqrt{3}$

B. $3\sqrt{3}$

C. $3\sqrt{4}$

D. $4\sqrt{16}$

Answer: A

Explanation: To solve this problem, the order of operations needs to be considered. In this problem, there are no operations within parenthesis that need to be performed, so the only step is to evaluate the operations as they appear from left to right following the operation rules. It is important to note that a negative exponent can become positive if the term that is being raised to the negative power is inversed ($x^{-1} = (1/x)^1$). The simplified results are:

$$\left(\frac{4}{5}\right)^2 \times 125 \times \frac{\sqrt{18 \times 2 + 3 \times 4}}{80} = \frac{16}{25} \times 125 \times \frac{\sqrt{36 + 12}}{80} = \sqrt{48} = \sqrt{16 \times 3} = 4\sqrt{3}$$

QUESTION 7

Joanna wants to enlarge the rectangular poster on her wall. She wants to enlarge the poster so it can have an area of 256 in², but wants the ratio of the height to the width to remain 1:4. What should the width of the enlarged poster be?

   A. 8

   B. 16

   C. 32

   D. Not enough information given to solve the problem

Answer: C

Explanation: To solve this problem, two equations need to be set up.

The first equation relates the area of a rectangular shape to the desired area of the poster.

$$256 = h \times w$$

The second equation relates the desired ratio between the height and the width of the poster.

$$\frac{h}{w} = \frac{1}{4}$$

The second equation can be solved for height in terms of width.

$$h = \frac{1}{4} \times w$$

Substituting the value of h into the first equation and solving for w yields 32 inches.

$$256 = \left(\frac{1}{4} \times w\right) \times w$$

$$256 = \left(\frac{w^2}{4}\right)$$

$$256(4) = w^2$$

$$1024 = w^2$$

$$w = \sqrt{1024} = 32 \text{ inches}$$

QUESTION 8

After a test, an instructor asked 5 students in the class how many hours they studied for the test. The students' responses are listed in the table below along with their test scores. What function, if any, describes the relationship between the hours studied and the score obtained by the students?

Student	Hours Studied	Exam Score
1	15	70
2	20	80
3	3	46
4	1	42
5	30	100

A. $e(h) = h^2 - 120$

B. $e(h) = 3h + 20$

C. $e(h) = 2h + 40$

D. None of the above

Answer: C

Explanation: The best approach to this problem is to use the answer choices given to determine if any could model the data supplied.

If 15 hours is substituted for h in answer choice A, a score of 105 results, which is not correct.

If 15 hours is substituted for h in answer choice B, a score of 65 results, which is not correct.

If 15 hours is substituted for h in answer choice C, a score of 70 results, which is correct. If the other 4 data points are tested with this equation, the correct answers result.

QUESTION 9

If Y is the dependent variable in the tables below, which of the following tables contains values that does not defines a function?

A

X	Y
5	123
8	510
12	1726
18	5830
23	12165

B

X	Y
-10	15
-5	10
0	5
5	10
10	15

C

X	Y
-10	913
-8	457
0	-7
16	-4391
24	-14455

D

X	Y
12	114
20	210
30	330
37	414
37	444

Answer: D

Explanation: For a function to be defined, there must be only one unique value of the dependent variable for any value in the domain of the function. In the tables shown above, only answer choice D fails to satisfy this requirement.

122

QUESTION 10

What value(s) of x are NOT included in the domain of this function?

$$f(x) = \frac{x^2 + 5x - 14}{x^2 - 7x + 10}$$

A. $x = -2, x = -5$

B. $x = 7$

C. $x = -5$

D. $x = 2, x = 5,$ and $x = -7$

Answer: A

Explanation: The domain of a function includes all values of the independent variable which will not result in an undefined value for the dependent variable. Undefined values occur if the denominator of a function is equal to 0. Thus, values of x which are not defined in the domain will include those values of x which result in the denominator equaling to 0. To solve this problem, the denominator is set equal to 0, and the values of x are solved for. $x^2 + 7x + 10 = 0$ results in $x = -2$ and $x = -5$. These two values of x will not be included in the domain of the function.

QUESTION 11

A cable connects the top of a post with the ground as shown in the figure below. The distance between the base of the tower and the base of the cable is 36 feet, and the cable has an angle of elevation of 35° with respect to the ground.

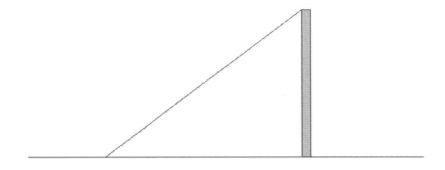

Note: Figure not drawn to scale.

What is the approximate height in feet of the post?

    A. 17

    B. 20

    C. 22

    D. 25

Answer: D

Explanation: The post is opposite to the angle of 35°. Therefore, one can use the sine function.

$$\sin(35°) = \frac{h}{36}$$

h is the height, and dimensions are in feet.

$$h = 36\sin(35°) = 25.2$$

QUESTION 12

Which of the following functions cannot be classified as an even function?

A. $|x| + 3 = f(x)$

B. $x^2 + 3 = f(x)$

C. $x^4 + 3 = f(x)$

D. $x + 3 = f(x)$

Answer: D

Explanation: An even function is defined as one in which the substitution of –x for x will result in the same value of the dependent variable as substitution of x would result in. In equation form, this is expressed as $(f(-x) = f(x))$. In the equations shown, substitution of –x into $|x|$, x^2, and x^4 would result in the same value as substitution of x would result in because the absolute value of a negative number is the positive number and raising a negative number to an even integer results in a positive output. Thus, the only equation which cannot be defined as an even function is in answer choice D.

QUESTION 13

Given that points I, J, and K represent the midpoints for their respective sides on ΔABC, what is the perimeter of triangle ABC?

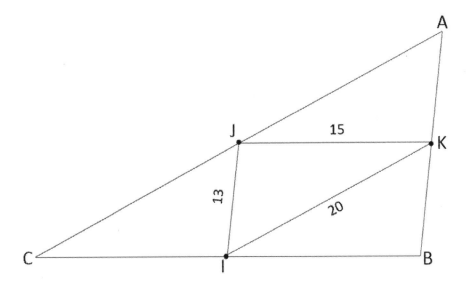

A. 48

B. 72

C. 96

D. 108

Answer: C

Explanation: The problem states the points I, J, and K were midpoints for their respective sides on ΔABC. The line segment formed by points I and K represent a mid-segment, so it will be half of the length of the line segment parallel to it, which is line segment AC. Line segment AC is 2 times the length of line segment IK (20). The same relationships can be used to derive the lengths of line segments BC and AB. The length of AC is 20 × 2=40, length of CB is 15 × 2=30, and length of AB is 13 × 2=26. These three lengths result in a perimeter of 96.

QUESTION 14

In parallelogram ABCD (not shown), ∢B = x + 15 and ∢C = 3x + 5. Which of the following statements regarding the diagonals of the parallelogram is true?

A. $\overline{BD} = \overline{CA}$

B. $\overline{BD} < \overline{CA}$

C. $\overline{BD} > \overline{CA}$

D. Not enough information given

Answer: C

Explanation: To understand the relative size of the two diagonals, it is necessary to know the size of the angles of the parallelogram.

The angle measures can be solved for with the given expressions for angles B and C. Angles B and C are consecutive angles in the parallelogram, so they are supplementary with each other. This allows for the two expressions given to be added and set equal to 180°. When this is done, the value of x derived is 40

$$x + 15 + 3x + 5 = 180$$

$$4x + 20 = 180$$

$$4x = 160$$

$$x = 40$$

Substituting 40 into the expressions for angles B and C results in values of 55 and 125, respectively. Thus, in the parallelogram ABCD, Angles C and A are the obtuse angles and Angles B and D are the acute angles. (Angle A is equal to Angle C because they are opposite to one another; this reasoning also explains the equivalence between Angles B and D).

One of the properties of a parallelogram is that the longer diagonal lies opposite the obtuse angle. If the obtuse angle is known to be Angle C, then the diagonal across will be the longer diagonal. This diagonal is line segment DB. Thus, $\overline{BD} > \overline{CA}$.

QUESTION 15

Which of the following statements accurately describes a rhombus?

    A. The diagonals of the quadrilateral are perpendicular

    B. The diagonals of the quadrilateral are congruent

    C. The diagonals of the quadrilateral bisect one another

    D. A and C

Answer: D

Explanation: To answer this question, it is necessary to know the properties of a rhombus. The important properties are listed below:

- Consecutive angles are supplementary
- Opposite angles are congruent
- Opposite sides are parallel to one another
- All sides are congruent
- Diagonals bisect the interior angles
- Diagonals are perpendicular bisectors

The last property implies that answer to the problem is D.

QUESTION 16

Which of the following line segment(s) represents a chord on the circle shown below?

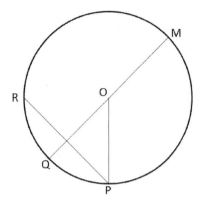

A. $\overline{RP}$

B. $\overline{PO}$

C. $\overline{MQ}$

D. A and C

Answer: D

Explanation: A chord is defined as a line segment that connects two points on the circumference of a circle. In the circle shown above, Points R and P are on the circumference, and a line segment connects the two points. Points M and Q are also on the circumference, and there is also a line segment that connects those two points. There are two chords shown in the circle, so the correct answer is D.

QUESTION 17

Which of the following scatter plots shows that there may be some degree of correlation between the dependent and independent variables?

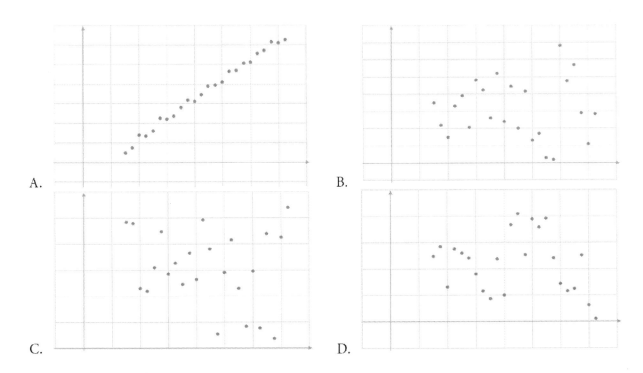

A.

B.

C.

D.

Answer: A

Explanation: A scatter plot can indicate a relationship among the two variables plotted if the points on the scatter plot line up to show a pattern. This is seen in option A. Option A indicates that as the value of the independent variable increases so will the value of the dependent variable.

QUESTION 18

When a six sided standard die is tossed once, what is the probability of getting 1, 3, and a 9?

A. $\frac{1}{6}$

B. $\frac{3}{6}$

C. 0

D. Undefined

Answer: C

Explanation: The first step is to list all the possible outcomes of rolling a six sided die. These outcomes are:

$$1 \quad 2 \quad 3 \quad 4 \quad 5 \quad 6$$

Of these outcomes, none of the outcomes have an option of 1, 3, and 9. Each outcome consists of only one single number, so the probability of getting a 1, 3, and a 9 is 0.

NOTE: This question for the probability of getting a 1, 3, and a 9 NOT the probability of getting a 1, 3, or 6.

QUESTION 19

Sets A and B are defined below. Which of the following sets represents A∩ B?

$$A = \{3, 6, 9, 12, 15, 18\}$$

$$B = \{2, 4, 6, 8, 10, 12, 14\}$$

A. {2, 3, 4, 6, 8, 9, 10, 12, 14, 15, 18}

B. 2, 3, 4, 6, 8, 9, 10, 12, 14, 15, 18

C. {6, 12}

D. A and B

Answer: C

Explanation: The symbol "∩" implies the intersection of the two sets. The intersection of two sets is defined as a set that contains all elements that both in A and B. In these two sets, the intersection would be set that contains the numbers 6 and 12.

QUESTION 20

A set has the following 10 numbers: 12, 19, 25, 28, 54, 26, 87, 23, 98, and 25. If an 11th number is to be added to the set, what does the number have to be in order for the set to have a mean of 40?

    A. -43

    B. 3

    C. 40

    D. 43

Answer: D

Explanation: For 11 numbers to have a mean of 40, the 11 numbers must add up to a value of 11 × 40=440. Currently, the 10 numbers add up to a value of 397. Thus, the 11th number must be 440 − 397=43.

QUESTION 21

A data set with a mean of 75 and a standard deviation of 3.5 is known to have a normal distribution. What percent of the data does NOT lie between 71.5 and 78.5?

    A. 99.95

    B. 68.2

    C. 31.8

    D. not enough information given

Answer: C

Explanation: The problem asks for what percent of the data does NOT lie between 71.5 and 78.5. It is important to note that 71.5 is equal to the mean minus the standard deviation and 78.5 is equal to the mean plus the standard deviation. Thus, the question is asking for the percent of the data that does not lie within one standard deviation of the mean.

In a normal distribution, 68.2% of the data lie within one standard deviation of the mean, which is an important fact to remember. Thus, the answer to the question is 31.8.

QUESTION 22

Which of the following ratios is not equal to 68%?

    A. 68:100

    B. 34:50

    C. 102:150

    D. 17:50

Answer: D

Explanation: Convert each ratio to decimal form to compare directly. All ratios, except D are equivalent to 0.68.

$$\frac{17}{50} = 0.34 = 34\%$$

QUESTION 23

Solve the following problem:

$$(5\text{-}1\times0+3\div3)\times\left(5+3\times2^4\right)\times\left(\dfrac{21\times3\times\dfrac{1}{7}}{5\text{-}1\times4\times3+2}\right)$$

    A. 0

    B. -572.4

    C. -230.4

    D. 57.24

Answer: B

Explanation: To solve this problem, the order of operations needs to be considered. In this problem, there are three separate groups of parenthesis. These must be evaluated in the proper order. The result is shown below:

$$(6)\times(53)\times\left(-\dfrac{9}{5}\right)$$

The next step is evaluating the remaining operations. The result is -572.4.

QUESTION 24

Chris' family drove a distance of 300 miles in 2 hours. Pat's family drove a distance of 400 miles in 3 hours. What is the ratio of the speed of Chris' family to the speed of Pat's family?

    A. 9/8

    B. 8/9

    C. 3/4

    D. 2/3

Answer: A

Explanation: To calculate the ratio between the two speeds, it is important to know the speed of Chris' family and the speed of Pat's family. Speed is taken to be the ratio of distance to time. Chris' family drove 300 miles in 2 hours, so their speed was 150 mph. Pat's family drove 400 miles in 3 hours, so their speed was $\frac{400}{3}$ mph. The ratio of the speed of Chris' family to the speed of Pat's family is $\frac{150}{\frac{400}{3}} = \frac{9}{8}$.

QUESTION 25

Which of the following represents the Commutative Property of Multiplication?

    A. $a \times b \times c = a \times b^c$

    B. $a \times b \times c = b \times c \times a$

    C. $a \times b \times c = a \times b \times c$

    D. $a \times b \times c = a + b + c$

Answer: B

Explanation: The Commutative Property of Multiplication states that the multiplication of numbers does not depend on the order in which the numbers are multiplied. In answer choice B, the order of the numbers is changed, but the numbers remain the same, which demonstrates the commutative property.

QUESTION 26

What are the values for the domain in the graph shown below?

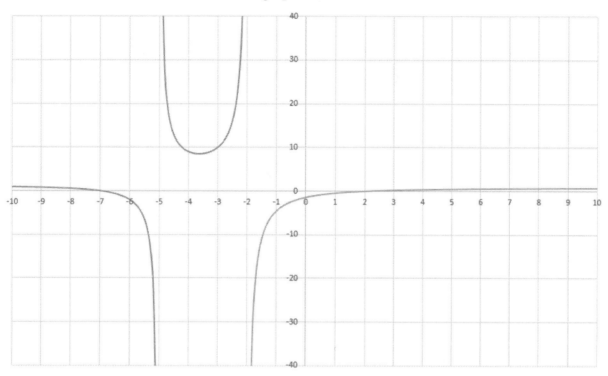

A. $[-5, -2]$

B. $[-\infty, -5) \cup (-5, -2) \cup (-2, \infty]$

C. $(-\infty, -5) \cup [-5, -2] \cup (-2, \infty)$

D. None of the above

Answer: D

Explanation: The graph shows asymptotes at x = –5 and x = –2; these two values cannot be included in the domain for the graph shown above. This eliminates answer choices A and C. Answer choice B is not correct because a parenthesis should be used to for ± ∞ in the interval. Thus, there is no answer given for the domain of this graph. The correct answer would be: $(-\infty, -5) \cup (-5, -2) \cup (-2, \infty)$

QUESTION 27

Which of the following is NOT equivalent to the radical below?

$$\sqrt[3]{324}$$

A. $3 \times \sqrt[3]{12}$

B. $\left(\dfrac{1}{324}\right)^{-\frac{1}{3}}$

C. $\left((324)^2\right)^{\frac{1}{6}}$

D. 18

Answer: D

Explanation: The best approach to this problem is to evaluate each option choice given and to see whether or not it equals the expression given.

To determine if the first option is equivalent to the expression given, it is necessary to input 3^3 into the radical $\sqrt[3]{12}$. This results in $\sqrt[3]{12 \times 27} = \sqrt[3]{324}$, which is equivalent to the expression given.

Option B is equivalent to the expression given. It is just expressed in a different format.

To determine if the third option is equivalent to the expression given, it is necessary to multiply the two exponent, which results in an exponent of 1/3. The originally expression had 324 raised to an exponent of 1/3, so this option is equivalent to the expression given.

If a calculator is used to evaluate the original expression, it would result in a value of 6.87 not 18. Thus, the third option is incorrect.

QUESTION 28

Of the following equations, which equation has an x – intercept greater than the y – intercept and a slope equal to the absolute value of the y – intercept.

    A. $y = 2x - 2$

    B. $y = 4x - 16$

    C. $y = 0.5x - 0.5$

    D. A and C

Answer: D

Explanation: The best approach to this problem is to determine the x – intercept, y – intercept, and slope for each option supplied. In the standard form of a linear equation ($y = mx + b$), b is the y – intercept and m is the slope. The x intercept is calculated by substituting the value of 0 for y and solving for x.

Answer choice A: $m = 2$, $b = -2$, and x – intercept is 1

> This answer is correct because the slope is equal to the absolute value of the y-intercept, and the x-intercept is greater than the y intercept

Answer choice B: $m = 4$, $b = -16$, and x – intercept is 4

> This answer is not correct because slope is not equal to the absolute value of the y intercept.

Answer choice C: $m = 0.5$, $b = -0.5$, and x – intercept is 1

> This answer is correct because the slope is equal to the absolute value of the y-intercept and the x intercept is greater than the y intercept.

Both answer choices A and C satisfy the constraints of the problem statement, so the correct answer is D.

QUESTION 29

What would be the y-intercept of the graph?

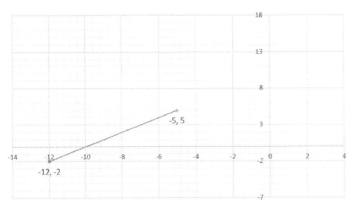

A. 13

B. 10

C. -14

D. -10

Answer: B

Explanation: The first step is to determine what the equation of the line is.

Since two points are known, the best approach is the point slope formula, which is: $y - y_1 = m \times (x - x_1)$. The variable m is the slope of the line, which can be calculated with the formula shown below.

$$m = \frac{y_2 - y_1}{x_2 - x_1}$$

The slope is calculated to be $\frac{-2 - 5}{-12 - -5} = 1$. Inputting this value for m and the known coordinate values into the point slope formula, the equation of the line is:

$$y-5=1(x-(-5))$$

$$y-5=1(x+5))$$

$$y-5+5=x+5+5$$

$$y=x+10$$

The next step is to determine the y intercept of the line. This is done by inputting a value of 0 for x into the equation of the line. This results in a value of 10. Thus, the y-intercept for a line is 10.

QUESTION 30

The table below shows the length of time in minutes 25 drivers were stuck in traffic during rush hour. Which of the following values cannot be determined from the data set shown below?

Time	Number of Drivers
0.0-5.5	3
5.5-15.5	10
15.5-25.5	8
25.5-30.5	1
30.5-45.5	3

A. range

B. mean

C. median

D. cannot be answered

Answer: D

Explanation: Without knowing the exact length of time, the range, mean, nor median cannot be calculated. It is necessary to know the exact time each driver was stuck in traffic, to calculate those three values.

QUESTION 31

A new ice cream store has opened, and the owner of the store has surveyed the first 100 customers. The survey showed that 67 customers have tried their homemade chocolate flavor and 82 customers have tried their homemade vanilla flavor. Of the 100 customers surveyed, 27 customers have tried the homemade vanilla flavor but not the homemade chocolate flavor. How many customers have tried neither the homemade vanilla flavor nor the homemade chocolate flavor?

A. 6

B. 12

C. 40

D. 55

Answer: A

Explanation: The best approach to this problem is to construct a Venn diagram. The total entire sample space consists of 100 customers. Of the 100 customers, 27 have tried only the homemade vanilla. It is known that a total of 82 have tried the homemade vanilla, so 55 of the 82 must have tried both homemade vanilla and homemade chocolate. If 55 have tried both homemade chocolate and homemade vanilla, then of the 67 customers who have tried homemade chocolate, 12 of them have tried only homemade chocolate. It is now known that 12 have tried only homemade chocolate, 27 have tried only homemade vanilla, and 55 have tried both homemade vanilla and homemade chocolate. This represents a total of 94 customers who have tried some type of ice cream at the store. Thus, only 6 customers have tried neither the homemade vanilla flavor nor the homemade chocolate flavor.

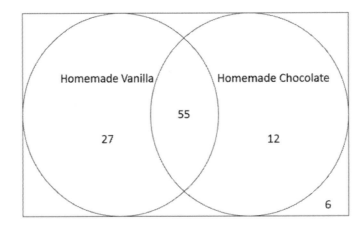

QUESTION 32

Mark and his wife are at the grand opening of a car dealership because they each want to win the two prizes that are being raffled away. Every attendee at the grand opening is allowed to write one name on a slip of paper and place that paper into a jar. Each attendee can get one prize. The manager will then select one name from the jar, and this person will have the option of choosing his or her prize. The manger will then select another name from the jar, and this person will take the remaining prize. If Mark and his wife have counted a total of 320 slips in the jar, what is the probability that they will each go home with a prize.

A. 9.80×10^{-6}

B. 6.25×10^{-3}

C. 9.77×10^{-6}

D. 1.96×10^{-5}

Answer: D

Explanation: The problem statement gives enough information to conclude the events of Mark and his wife receiving a prize are dependent because once the first slip is drawn, the number of remaining slips in the jar will decrease.

The first probability necessary to calculate is the probability that either Mark or his wife is called first. The probability the Mark's name will be called in the first raffle is $\frac{1}{320}$. The probability that his wife's name will be called in the first raffle is $\frac{1}{320}$. The probability that Mark or his wife receive the first gift is $\frac{1}{320} + \frac{1}{320} = \frac{2}{320}$. If Mark or his wife are the recipients of the first raffle, then the probability that the other receives the second raffle is $\frac{1}{319}$. The denominator is reduced by 1 because the slip of the first recipient is not replaced back in the jar. The probability that Mark and his wife each go home with a prize is $\frac{2}{320} \times \frac{1}{319} = 1.96 \times 10^{-5}$.

QUESTION 33

Which of the following events are mutually exclusive?

    A. The event of a getting an odd number and an even number when a single card is drawn from a deck.

    B. The event of getting a 3 and an odd number when a die is tossed.

    C. The event of getting 7 and a number less than 9 when a single card is drawn from a deck.

    D. The event of getting a 5 and a number less than 6 when a die is tossed.

Answer: A

Explanation: To answer this question, it is important to know the definition of mutually exclusive events. Mutually exclusive events are those events which cannot happen simultaneously. To answer this question, it is necessary to determine whether each even in the four options can happen at the same time.

In option A, it is impossible to draw a card that has a number that is both even and odd. Thus, these two events are mutually exclusive, and this is the correct answer.

In option B, it is possible to get a 3 and an odd number when a die is tossed because 3 is an odd number.

In option C, it is possible to get a 7 and a number less than 9 when a single card is drawn because 7 is less than 9.

In option D, it is possible to get 5 and a number less than 6 when a die is tossed because 5 is less than 6.

QUESTION 34

On a school field trip, Timothy has to choose a walking buddy to accompany him to the vending machine. Of the thirty students he can choose from, 20 are older than him and 10 are younger than him. Of the 20 students older than Timothy, 12 are boys, and of the 10 students younger than him, 6 are girls. What is the probability that Timothy chooses a walking buddy that is older than him or a boy?

- A. $\frac{6}{5}$
- B. $\frac{2}{3}$
- C. $\frac{4}{5}$
- D. $\frac{11}{15}$

Answer: C

Explanation: The first step is to determine whether the events of choosing student older than him and a boy are mutually exclusive. Since there are 12 boys older than Timothy, the two events are not mutually exclusive.

Since the events are not mutually exclusive, the probably that either one may occur is the sum of the probabilities of each occurring separately minus the probably of both happening simultaneously. This can be expressed as:

P (older or boy) = P (older) + P (boy) – P (older and boy)

The probability of selecting a student older than Timothy is $\frac{20}{30} = \frac{2}{3}$

The probability of selecting a student that is a boy is $\frac{16}{30} = \frac{8}{15}$. The 16 resulted from the 12 boys older than him and the 4 boys younger than him.

The probability of selecting an older boy is $\frac{12}{30} = \frac{2}{5}$

Inputting these probabilities into the equation above results in a probability of $\frac{24}{30} = \frac{4}{5}$

QUESTION 35

Which of the following situations describes dependent events?

    A. The probability of selecting a quarter from a piggy bank and then selecting a penny.

    B. The probability of getting 3 from a single toss of a die and then another 3 from another toss of the die.

    C. The probability of selecting a quarter from a piggy bank and then selecting a penny after the quarter has been put back.

    D. A and C

Answer: A

Explanation: To solve this problem, the definition of dependent events needs to be known. Dependent events are those events where the outcome of one the events affects the probability of the other event(s).

In option A, the first quarter is not replaced, so when the penny is selected, its sample space is reduced. The sample space for the penny after the selection of the quarter is not the same as the sample space for the selection of the penny without the selection of the quarter before it. Thus, these are dependent events.

In option B, the sample space for tossing a die stays constant and is independent of how many times the die has already been tossed. Thus, these events are not dependent on one another.

In option C, the quarter has been put back into the piggy bank after it has been chosen. The sample space for the penny after the selection of the quarter is the same as the sample space for the selection of the penny before the selection of the quarter. Thus, these events are not dependent on one another.

QUESTION 36

A shoe store receives a weekly shipment of 100 shoes on Sunday night, so that it can have full inventory to sell from on Monday morning. In a certain week, the store manager was notified that the shipment for that week contained 5 shoes that were damaged due to mishandling. If this notification came Tuesday, and 5 of the 100 delivered shoes were sold the previous day (Monday), what is the probability that at least 1 of the 5 shoes sold was damaged?

A. 0.05

B. 0.230

C. 0.770

D. 0.95

Answer: B

Explanation: The first step is to determine the number of different ways in which 5 of the 100 shoes can be sold. The counting principle can be used to find this number, but it would be too tedious. The best approach is to use the combinations rule. The combinations rule is used because the order in which the 5 shoes were sold does not matter. The combination rule states that number of possibilities of arranging r objects selected from n objects is calculated by:

$$_nC_r = \frac{n!}{(n-r)! \times r!}$$

Using the above formula, with $_{100}C_5$, the total number of ways of selling 5 shoes from a total number of 100 shoes is 75,287,520.

To find the probability that at least 1 of the 5 shoes is damaged, it is best to first calculate the probability of zero damaged shoes being sold. If it is known that 5 shoes are damaged, then it is also known that 95 shoes are not damaged. The total number of ways of selling 5 of these 95 shoes is calculated to be 57,940,519 ($_{95}C_5$). The probability of selling 0 damaged shoes is $\frac{57,940,519}{75,287,520} = 0.770$. The probability that at least 1 of the 5 shoes that are sold is damaged is 1 − 0.770=0.230.

Of all the outcomes in the sample space for selling the 5 shoes, there is only one outcome in which at least 1 damaged shoe is not sold, and this outcome is where zero damaged shoes are sold. Thus, subtracting the probability of zero damaged shoes being sold from the probability of the entire sample space (1), the probability of at least one damaged shoe being sold is derived.

QUESTION 37

Coach Johnson tells his quarterback to stand 50 yards away from the poster shown below, and throw the football at the shaded circle. The intention of this drill is to improve the accuracy of the quarterback's throws. If the quarterback's throw hits the poster, what is the probability that it will hit the shaded circle?

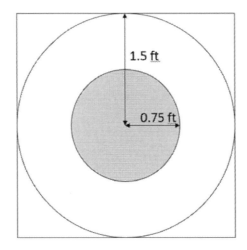

A. 0.196

B. 0.250

C. 0.520

D. 0.785

Answer: A

Explanation: To answer this question, the area of the poster and the shaded circle need to be known. The area of the poster is the area of a square of length 3 ft; the area is calculated to be 9ft². The area of the shaded circle is $0.75^2 \times \pi = 1.76715$ ft². The probability that the football hits the shaded circle is 1.76715/9=0.196.

QUESTION 38

Of the equations below, which equation does NOT have an x–intercept of 5 and a y–intercept of 15?

    A. $y = -3x + 15$

    B. $y + 15 = -2 \times (x - 15)$

    C. $2y = -6x + 30$

    D. $y - 9 = -3 \times (x - 2)$

Answer: B

Explanation: The best approach is to determine the x intercept and y-intercept of each option. The x-intercept is the value of x that will result in a value of 0 for y. The y-intercept is the value of y when x is equal to 0.

The linear equation in option A is written in standard form: $y = mx + b$, were b is the y-intercept. Thus, the y-intercept for option A is 15. The x-intercept is calculated to be 5.

The linear equation in option B is written in point slope form: $y - y_1 = m (x - x_1)$. To determine the y intercept, a value of 0 is substituted for x, and the equation is solved for y. The result is a y intercept of 15. The x-intercept is calculated by substituting 0 for y and solving for x. The result is 7.5. Since the x-intercept is not equal to 5, this is the answer.

QUESTION 39

Which of the following line(s) represents an axis of symmetry for $y = 6x^2 + 24x - 24$?

    A. $x = -2$

    B. $x = -2$ and $y = -24$

    C. $x = 2$

    D. $x = 0$

Answer: A

Explanation: The axis of symmetry is a line that passes through the vertex of a parabola, and cuts the parabola into two mirror halves. To determine the line of symmetry, it is important to first calculate the vertex of the parabola.

The quadratic equation given is the standard form ($y = ax^2 + bx + c$). The vertex of a parabola given in this form is $-\frac{b}{2a}$. The axis of symmetry will be a vertical line because only a vertical line can equally divide the parabola into two mirror halve. This line of symmetry will be a vertical line passing through the vertex of the parabola, so its equation will be $x = -\frac{b}{2a}$; this is calculated to be $x = -2$.

QUESTION 40

Which of the following expressions is equivalent to the expression below?

$$\left(\frac{6\text{-}x}{5x\text{-}30}\right)^{-1} \times \left(\frac{5yx+5y}{10yx+5yx}\right)$$

A. $\dfrac{(x+1)}{15x}$

B. $\dfrac{-5y(x+6)}{3x}$

C. $\dfrac{-5(x+1)}{3x}$

D. $\dfrac{3(x+1)}{5}$

Answer: C

Explanation: The first approach is to determine the factors of each expression in the numerators and denominators. This is shown below:

$$\left(\frac{6\text{-}x}{5(x\text{-}6)}\right)^{-1} \times \left(\frac{5y(x+1)}{5yx(2+1)}\right)$$

The next step is to take into account the negative exponent. The best way to handle a negative exponent is to flip entire expression. This is shown below:

$$\left(\frac{5(x\text{-}6)}{6\text{-}x}\right) \times \left(\frac{5y(x+1)}{5yx(2+1)}\right)$$

The next step is to cancel any common factors that are in the numerator and denominator. This is shown below:

$$\left(\frac{\cancel{5}(x\text{-}6)}{6\text{-}x}\right) \times \left(\frac{5\cancel{y}(x+1)}{\cancel{5y}x(2+1)}\right)$$

The expression remaining can be simplified. The simplified result is shown below.

$$\left(\frac{(x\text{-}6)}{6\text{-}x}\right) \times \left(\frac{5(x+1)}{x(2+1)}\right) = \left(\frac{\text{-}(6\text{-}x)}{6\text{-}x}\right) \times \left(\frac{5(x+1)}{x(3)}\right) = \left(\frac{\text{-}\cancel{(6\text{-}x)}}{\cancel{6\text{-}x}}\right) \times \left(\frac{5(x+1)}{x(3)}\right) = \frac{\text{-}5(x+1)}{3x}$$

Constructed Response 1

Use the data provided to complete the task that follows.

Using the data provided, prepare a response of approximately 400–600 words in which you:

- identify an important mathematical strength related to the standard that is demonstrated by the student, citing specific evidence from the exhibits to support your assessment;
- identify an important area of need related to the standard that is demonstrated by the student, citing specific evidence from the exhibits to support your assessment; and
- describe an instructional plan that builds on the student's strengths and that would help the student improve in the identified area of need. Include a plan for assisting the student build a viable argument related to the given standard.

Eighth-grade students have been developing their understanding functions and modeling relationships between quantities. The class is currently working on the following standard from the New York State P–12 Common Core Learning Standards for Mathematics:

CCSS.Math.Content.8.F.A.3

Interpret the equation $y = mx + b$ as defining a linear function, whose graph is a straight line; give examples of functions that are not linear.

Description of Class Activity

A father is considering two options to give an allowance at the end of each month to his teenage son for 12 months, provided the son completes all his house chores. The two options are:

Option 1: Receive $20 at the end of the first month. Every month thereafter receive 15% more than the previous month.

Option 2: Receive $50 at the end of the first month. Every month thereafter receive $1 more than the allowance of the previous month.

Use your knowledge of exponential and linear functions to develop a response in which you analyze the allowance received each month during a 12-month period under each option. In your response:

G. create a data table representing the allowance received each month over a 12-month period for each option;
H. graph the data from both tables on the same coordinate grid and connect the data with the line or curve that best fits the data;
I. compare the allowance plans over the 12-month period, including a discussion of the significance of the point of intersection of the two graphs;
J. explain what type of function, exponential or linear, models each option;
K. find equations that describe each option; and
L. identify an expression that represents the difference between the allowances received under the two options in the twelfth month.

Be sure to show your work and explain the reasoning you use in analyzing and solving this problem.

Excerpt of Student's Work

Part A

The tables representing the allowances received each month over the 12-month period for the two options are shown below.

Option 1

Month	1	2	3	4	5	6	7	8	9	10	11	12
Allowance ($)	20	23	26.45	30.42	34.98	40.23	46.26	53.2	61.18	70.36	80.91	93.05

Each new value is obtained by taking the previous month and adding the 15% of the previous month. This is shown below.

New Value=Previous Month Value+15% of Previous Month Value

For the second month, the calculation is shown next.

New Value=20+0.15(20)=20+3=23

Other values are obtained similarly.

Option 2

Month	1	2	3	4	5	6	7	8	9	10	11	12
Allowance ($)	50	51	52	53	54	55	56	57	58	59	60	61

Part D

Option 1 shows a curve that is linear up until month 9, where it starts to become steeper as time goes by. Therefore, it is an exponential function.

Option 2 shows a constant increase of $1. Therefore, it is a linear function.

Excerpt of Conversation With Teacher

Teacher: How did you find the equation for Option 1?

Student: I used the standard slope formula.

Teacher: What is that formula?

Student: y=mx+b

Teacher: Why did you use this formula?

Student: Because there is almost a constant change, so that is the best way to write equation.

Teacher: How did you use this formula to write the equation?

Student: I took two points. I used two points to find the slope. Then, used the slope and one coordinate to find the formula.

Teacher: Is there any other way that you can find the equation?

Student: I don't think so.

NOTE: Note: To receive individualized feedback, email essay to onlinepreparationservices@gmail.com and allow 5-7 days for feedback

NYSTCE® Field 232 Multi-Subject: Teachers of Middle Childhood Grade 5–Grade 9

New York State Teacher Certification Examinations®

This page is intentionally left blank.

Made in the USA
Middletown, DE
07 August 2020